LORIN C. WOOLLEY'S

SCHOOL OF THE PROPHETS

MINUTES FROM 1932-1941

First Edition - First Printing

Edited by
DREW BRINEY, J.D.

ABBREVIATIONS:

Minutes Prophets:	Lorin C. Woolley's School of the Minutes from 1932-1941
JD	Journal of Discourses
MS	Millennial Star
HC	History of the Church
D&C	Doctrine and Covenants: Utah edition
TPJS	Teachings of the Prophet Joseph Smith
WJS	Words of Joseph Smith

© Copyright 2009 by Hindsight Publications, llc
All rights reserved. Published in the United States by Hindsight Publications, llc.

TABLE OF CONTENTS

PREFACE

NOTES ON EDITING

Editing this small volume proved to be more work than anticipated. Initially, the vast majority of the following minutes were in code. In fact, there were two codes used by the scriveners. One code named each member of the council as 5, 10, 15, 20, etc. but the numbers were not listed in order of seniority. The other code appears to have been a random arrangement of numbers and letters that must have had a key to decipher the code somewhere else. The original manuscript that was made available to the editor by Ivan Nielsen had handwritten notes that revealed the code names of several individuals. Throughout this volume, the code has been replaced with names (or nouns as the case may have been) with only a few exceptions. The first set of exceptions is when sensitive family information about individuals was included in the original minutes. In these few cases, the code remains even when the names of some of these individuals is known. The second set of exceptions is when the code's decipher was not written in the original manuscript made available to the editor or when the handwriting was so faint that no intelligent guess could be made as to what the handwriting said.

The scrivener appears to have changed some time in 1935 and perhaps a time or two thereafter. Accordingly, the grammar of the minutes changed, the format changed, and the usage and frequency of abbreviations changed. Because the original and official minutes were typewritten, these changes appear to be issues of expediency and not issues of writing styles. To make the text more easily readable, punctuation, format, and abbreviations have all been standardized without any notice thereof in the text. Nevertheless, throughout the minutes, there is no editing that makes a substantive or contextual change. If there was any questions as to whether or not a change would be substantive rather than stylistic, no change was made. In furtherance of that effort, the reader will note that there are several instances where stylistic capitalizations have been carried over from the original: Apostle, Patriarchal Order, Sacrament, Sectarian, and other clear efforts to capitalize words that held special meaning to the scrivener have been retained throughout this volume.

Apparently for purposes of brevity, many entries are not written in complete sentences. Consequently, the scrivener or scriveners became somewhat excessive in the use of commas to separate phrases. When context and meaning was clear and unambiguous, the editor deleted many unnecessary commas – only occasionally were clearly missing punctuation marks added in the main text. Although these grammar, format, and abbreviation issues required many, many changes to create an easily read volume, the editor believes that no substantive changes have been made in any instance – all changes have been technical as described above. Lastly – and without altering the ordering of any portion of the minutes – technical, administrative details have been grouped closely together so that the casual reader can read through the historical and doctrinal materials more quickly (skimming the technicalities) – and without stumbling through where the meeting was held, who opened, who blessed the sacrament, etc. Similarly, extra hard returns were added to separate different issues that were discussed during a single meeting.

As is customary, brackets "[abc]" represent insertions not in the original text and parentheses "(abc)" represent either parenthetical phrases originally separated by commas or punctuation found in the original manuscript.

With the code largely deciphered, with abbreviations completed, and with punctuation, spelling, and format standardized, the following materials should be relatively easy to read and the reader should be able to easily focus on the interesting details surrounding the history and doctrine of Lorin C. Woolley's original council of friends.

INTRODUCTION

OBSERVATIONS FROM THE MINUTES

Up until the present time, very few people have had access to the minutes of the meetings held by Lorin C. Woolley's school of the prophets and none of them have been published for historical inspection, review, or casual reading for the curious. The following summary constitutes observations outlining the transition from Lorin C. Woolley's original council of friends to the germination of the various fundamentalist groups that trace their priesthood lineage through Lorin C. Woolley. The meeting minutes are therefore not only relevant to Woolley's priesthood claims, they are also directly relevant to the birth of the most prominent practitioners of Mormon plural marriage anywhere since Mormonism first appeared in the early nineteenth century.

The meetings first began on September 1, 1932 in the home of J. Leslie Broadbent in Salt Lake City.[1] Weekly meetings for the newly called school of the prophets usually vacillated between this home and Joseph Musser's office, which was also located in Salt Lake City. The meetings typically began with the administration of the sacrament using unleavened bread and wine and members of the council took turns conducting based upon their seniority in ordination.[2] Soon after the meetings began, Lorin Woolley became ill and was thereafter unable to attend most of the meetings before he died on September 19, 1934. However, because Joseph Musser was fairly conscientious about keeping a record of Woolley's teachings, a summary of those teachings are included at the beginning of the record. This summary extends from September 1, 1932 until January 11, 1934.

Two themes found within the minutes are of particular interest. First, after the school of the prophets

---

1 J. Leslie Broadbent was Lorin Woolley's undisputed successor in the council. The first recorded meeting however was on January 18, 1934.

2 See *Minutes* 1a.

began its formal meetings, each of the new council members began making diligent efforts to have their ordinations to the "Priesthood of Elijah" completed. They believed that these ordinations were incomplete until the Savior personally anointed their heads and then personally sealed those anointings in accordance with the teachings of early LDS prophets.[3] The minutes leave no question but that they believed that their appointment to this apostleship was incomplete until this sacred privilege had been received by the worthy candidate.[4]

Noting that none of these new apostles had fulfilled this appointment as of March 16, 1938, one new member queried: "Is it possible the Priesthood is out of order as is the

---

3 See *Minutes* 95b. Lorin C. Woolley elsewhere taught: "You must know Jesus Christ, personally, while in this probation." *Reminiscences* 1:6 (A Discussion with Carl Jentzsch). He also testified to Ferrell Coombs that he could trace his priesthood authority directly to Christ. *See Id.* 1:11.
Joseph Smith taught the same thing. In *TPJS*, 180, we read that "All the prophets had the Melchizedek Priesthood and were ordained by God himself." Despite this unequivocal statement, Oliver Cowdery's observation on this matter is perhaps the most famous among LDS Church history buffs:

[I]t is necessary that you ... can bear testimony ... that you have seen the face of God. ... Your ordination is not full and complete till God has laid his hand upon you. We require as much to qualify us as did those who have gone before us. God is the same. If the Savior in former days laid His hands on His disciples, why not in the latter days? ... [B]ear this testimony, that you have seen the face of God ... for it is your duty and your privilege to bear such testimony for yourselves. HC 2:195 (2/4/1835); RLDSCH 1:546.

When Lorenzo Snow was set apart as president of the LDS Church, his blessing stated that he had already received the apostleship "through your Lord and Savior Jesus Christ." *Journal History of the Church* (10/10/1898) as cited in See Anderson, J. Max, *Mormon Fundamentalism: A Study in the Foundational Claims of Contemporary Polygamous Sub-Cultures*, unpublished manuscript of his book, copy in author's possession (hereinafter, *Anderson*), Lorenzo Snow, 4-5. See also *JD* 9:87. The wording of the second anointing confirms this injunction as delivered by Oliver Cowdery. See also, *Eloheim at the Altar: The Rituals and Ceremonies of the Mormon Priesthood,* (under the pen name of Bojamah Azkin), Special Collections, University of Utah, 115-16; *MS* 14:690, 691; *A Priesthood Issue*, 23 (the pamphlet was originally printed in *Truth* 5:179 #8.); *Joseph W. Musser's Book of Remembrance*, 24.
4 See *Minutes* 115b. While they believed that they had proper authority, they believed that their "appointment" to exercise that authority was incomplete. See *Minutes* 7b. This appointment was to be "set apart to receive revelations and special direction on specified subjects, which revelations, after being approved by the mouthpiece of God, are made official." See *Minutes* 9a.

Church?"[5] Because this capstone ordnance was of such great importance, the minutes are peppered with the council's efforts to obtain these blessings. They regularly fasted from food, water, and intimate relations with their wives and they regularly participated in formal prayer circles. In these prayer circles, they occasionally each prayed in turn "for a confirmation from heaven of their calling," sometimes using signs taught in the Mormon temple endowment but always considering a "confirmation and actual knowledge" the "foremost blessing sought after."[6] This continued until roughly mid-1941 when the meeting minutes abruptly end.[7]

This "Apostleship"[8] was of such monumental significance to this first council that they lamented Lorin C. Woolley's passing in part, because he was, "according to [their] understanding the only mortal man left who actually knew the Lord Jesus Christ and was anointed by Him."[9] After his passing, the council viewed the ensuing period as "times of uncertainty."[10] Though the council had "a senior, no one [had] been designated by the Lord as the 'one man'" spoken of in D&C 132:7.[11] Thus, while the senior council member was honored and respected for his position of seniority in the council, they did not consider his senior ordination equivalent to the honor of being designated the

---

[5] See *Minutes* 108b. References stating or suggesting that no one had received the second comforter or its accompanying ordinances as outlined above are found on the majority of minute meeting pages. See also *Reminiscences* 1:4 (A Discussion with William Thomas)("the Council was never fully organized"); 1:10 (A Discussion with Olive Woolley Coombs)("The Kingdom of God not the Church is to be set in order;" alternatively, the Church, the kingdom, and the Council of Friends would all be out of order).

[6] See *Minutes* 2b, 12b, 30b, 34b, 39b, 45b, 51b, 56b, 58b (where a council member prays for Broadbent to be given this knowledge), 59b, 68b (where they united "their faith and prayers ... for deliverance from Spiritual and financial bondage."), 97b, 110b, and 115b.

[7] Presumably, there are more meeting minutes held by fundamentalists but those minutes would either lead quickly into "the split" or start right after "the split," which happened shortly thereafter.

[8] Apostleship with a capitalized "A" apparently distinguishes their understanding of their office from the office of other apostleships.

[9] See *Minutes* 8a, 45b, 50b, 97b, and 115b. See also *Reminiscences* 1:11.

[10] See *Minutes* 43b.

[11] See *Minutes* 97b. However, note that Lorin Woolley taught that the keys of the Priesthood were "held by the senior in ordination of the seven" – an allusion to the "one man" doctrine. See *Joseph W. Musser's Book of Remembrance*, 48.

"one man" with all of the sealing keys until he had received his personal visitation, anointing, ordination, and appointment from Jesus Christ himself. This initial set of minutes offers no record of any member of the council receiving a completed appointment but two entries in early 1934 mention that several members of their congregations "testified that the face or likeness of the Savior overshadowed J. Leslie Broadbent's countenance."[12]

The nature of the authority of this apostleship is also of interest. Lorin Woolley informed the council that they were acting as officers of the "Kingdom in this dispensation."[13] He further taught them that the "Grand Council" of this "Kingdom of God" was fully completed and organized in the winter of 1843-44 by the prophet Joseph Smith "when the Grand Council was fully completed."[14] This Grand Council of the kingdom was to hold keys "possessed by the group as a body, their powers being expressed through" the "one man" designated by the Lord or "such other party as the group may designate."[15] They further claimed that their "united voice on a question in line with [their] responsibility and duty is the word of the Lord on the subject."[16]

---

12 See *Minutes* 9b, 18b. See also *Diary of Joseph Lyman Jessop Journal*, (No publication information: no date; circa 1993-98), Vol. 2 January 1 1934 to April 21, 1945, (Hereinafter: *Joseph Lyman Jessop Journal*), (4/8/1934). Compare this with the August 8, 1844 transfiguration of Brigham Young during the succession crisis. Quinn, D. Michael, *The Mormon Hierarchy: Origins of Power*, (Signature Books: 1994) 167 (hereinafter, *Origins*), Welch, John W., ed., *Opening the Heavens: Accounts of Divine Manifestations 1820-1844*, (Brigham Young University Press: 2005), 373-480.

13 See *Minutes* 3a.

14 See *Minutes* 9a (See also 3a); see also *Joseph W. Musser's Book of Remembrance*, 44. The term "Grand Council of the Kingdom of God" was used by Joseph Fielding on April 18, 1844 to refer to the Council of Fifty. *Origins*, 358. Quinn notes that the term "Grand Council ... did not uniquely apply to the Council of Fifty, since it was a term in the mid-1830s for a joint meeting of stake leaders and general authorities." *Origins*, 359. Joseph also used the term "Grand Council" many times in connection with a council of the Gods. For a small sampling, see Ehat, Andrew F. and Cook, Lindon W., eds., *Words of Joseph Smith: The Contemporary Accounts of the Nauvoo Discourses of the Prophet Joseph*, (Religious Studies Center, BYU: 1990), 245, 341, 345, 351, 353, 358-69, 362, 267, 370 (Hereinafter: *WJS*).

15 See *Minutes* 95b, 97b.

16 See *Minutes* 97b.

The references to the "Kingdom of God [being] organized in the winter of 1843-44 by Joseph Smith, when the Grand Council was fully completed" is both confusing and quite helpful. It is confusing because the statement could be read to mean that the Kingdom of God was not organized until after the Grand Council had been created or it could be read to mean that the Kingdom of God was organized at the same time when, incidentally, the Grand Council was fully completed. The latter interpretation construes the comma in the original manuscript as the separation of an afterthought. The first interpretation construes the comma as a clause modifying the first clause. Given the grammatical patterns throughout the minutes, either construction is rationally defensible. From a historical standpoint, the ambiguity is almost distressing because the answer to this question would be quite helpful in definitively determining what Lorin C. Woolley understood to be the scope of authority held by this Grand Council.

The 1834-44 date informs us that he viewed the authority of this council to be connected to either the Quorum of Anointed (Church of the Firstborn) or the Council of Fifty. Because Lorin C. Woolley claimed that this council held the priesthood of Elijah – a clear allusion to the second anointing – the connection to the Quorum of Anointed is clear because the second anointing was restored within the organization of the Quorum of Anointed in September of 1843.

By March of 1844, the Council of Fifty was organized and this council was (and continues to be) commonly referred to as the kingdom of God. Because Lorin Woolley claimed to hold the "Keys of the Kingdom,"[17] his claim that he held the keys of the Council of Fifty is unmistakable. However, because he claims the "Kingdom of God was organized … when the Grand Council was fully completed," the question as to whether Woolley considered this Grand Council as a presiding quorum of the "Kingdom of God" is also unclear from the minutes.

---

[17] See *Minutes* 3a.

It is clear that the term "Grand Council of the Kingdom of God" was used by Lyman Wight when referring to the Nauvoo era Council of Fifty and that the term Grand Council was similarly used with regularity in connection with the Council of Fifty in Nauvoo.[18] However, the term was also used in connection with other councils in the 1830s so this terminology is not determinative.[19] Nevertheless, given many references to the priesthood of Elijah and similar terminology throughout Woolley-based fundamentalist literature, it is tempting to conclude that Woolley used and understood the kingdom rhetoric to refer to the keys of the kingdom held exclusively by the Church of the Firstborn (viz., the Holy Order, Joseph Smith's Quorum of Anointed, etc.).[20] However, this is not indisputable – and the minutes themselves offer no foolproof guidance.[21] Still, the connection seems plausible and other rhetoric employed in the minutes suggests that this connection is accurate.

Woolley further claims that he held the keys of the patriarchal order.[22] Since the "patriarchal order" is a very clear reference to temple ordinances,[23] and since that

---

18 *Origins*, 120, 358-59.
19 See *Origins*, 359.
20 See *Silencing Mormon Polygamy*, chapter 12 for a detailed discussion of these issues.
21 In *An Event of the Underground Days*, 8, Kingston refers to this "grand council of the kingdom" as "a secular organization consisting of fifty men," which could be read as a rejection of the proposed historical foundation for fundamentalist Mormon priesthood claims to the priesthood of Elijah. Nevertheless, the explanation found within Kingston's pamphlet does not authoritatively represent the teachings of Lorin C. Woolley (although it appears that Woolley approved of the content of the compilation of his testimony about 1886 events) and they do not appear consistent with some of Lorin C. Woolley's teachings as found in *Joseph W. Musser's Book of Remembrance* and in these school of the prophet minutes.
22 See *Minutes* 3a-4a. He did not claim to hold the keys to the presidency of the LDS Church despite his claim that they "never passed to Heber J. Grant."
23 For any reader unacquainted with this connection, see *WWJ* (3/4/1897); Ehat, Andrew F., *Joseph Smith's Introduction of Temple Ordinances and the 1844 Mormon Succession Question*; (December 1982), 142; *LDS Church Authority*, 14; and Quinn, D. Michael, "*the Mormon Succession Crisis of 1844*," BYU Studies, 16 (Winter 1976), 203. Joseph Fielding Smith also acknowledged this connection in: "*Speech before the Brigham Young Student Body*," (6/15/1956) when he stated that the "Patriarchal Priesthood will be the priesthood that will be held by all those worthy of exaltation in the Celestial Kingdom of God. For the whole plan of salvation and exaltation is based on the Patriarchal Order."

terminology was used by early fundamentalists to describe plural marriage,[24] and since the major impetus behind the 1886 ordinations was to keep plural marriages alive, it is tempting for the uninitiated reader to presume that Woolley was claiming that the keys of the patriarchal order included the authority to oversee and perform all temple ordinances, including the performance of plural marriages and the second anointing. That assessment is nevertheless incorrect. The minutes themselves offer no clear explanation of the nature of these keys but other sources indisputably confirm the fact that Woolley used these terms to refer to the office of the Church patriarch.[25]

The third key that Woolley claimed to possess was the keys of the Priesthood. These keys are never clearly addressed as such in the minutes themselves but they are found in the record. Nevertheless, from other sources, it is clear that these keys refer to the "one man" who presides over the Grand Council.[26]

The second theme of interest involves the evolution of authority exercised by the council. They felt "a duty to confine [their] activities to the labors appointed … in [their] ordination and succeeding instructions."[27] So long as they did not have anyone designated as the "one man," they decided to "give no instruction as a Priesthood without first counseling together and being united."[28] In consideration of

---

24 See Daniel Bateman's 1934 account and Byron Harvey Allred's 1925 account (*Silencing Mormon Polygamy: Failed Persecutions, Divided Saints, and the Rise of Mormon Fundamentalism*, Appendixes) for their references to the patriarchal order of marriage. See also *Wilford Woodruff's Journal* (12/31/1886) and *JD* 3:125.

25 If the *Minutes* were consistent, the list of who has held the keys in this dispensation would be more definitive. See *Minutes* 3a-4a. See also *Items from the Book of Remembrance*, 95; *Reminiscences* 3:3-4, 46-47; *Laman Manasseh Victorious*, 99. Musser also taught that these keys included the authority to preside over the Church. *Joseph W. Musser's Book of Remembrance*, 48.

26 *Joseph W. Musser's Book of Remembrance*, 48. *Items From the Book of Remembrance*, 27; *Reminiscences* 5:36-37. In turn, the Grand Council presides over the kingdom of God. Additionally, the holder of the keys of the Patriarchal Order presides over holder of the keys of the Presidency of the Church. *Joseph W. Musser's Book of Remembrance*, 48.

27 See *Minutes* 95b. See also *Minutes* 43b.

28 See *Minutes* 108b. See also *Minutes* 39b: [W]e are waiting for light and have gone about as far as we can go." The council was also "cautioned not to advance

these concerns, the council discussed many fundamental issues in their meetings before offering any counsel to members of their congregations. For instance, after receiving a request to give patriarchal blessings to a family, the council decided that it "functions, at present, only in those matters pertaining to life and salvation that cannot wait until the Church is set in order, nevertheless, let the Spirit be free in dictating the proper course to pursue." This, of course, is in harmony with John Taylor's injunctions as reported by Dan Bateman in 1934.[29]

Initially, the council declined to administer the sacrament to excommunicated members of the Church and further declined to regularly conduct private sacrament meetings.[30] They also informed followers that monies received would be received as donations, not as tithing, and they wanted "the Saints [to] understand it as such."[31] However, by March of 1934, the council was beginning to encourage members to privately baptize their children and to confirm them members of the Church of Jesus Christ of Latter-day Saints and to keep a personal record of these ordinances "to be reported for Church record at the proper time" – presumably when the LDS Church was to be set back in order.[32]

The first ordination to the priesthood (apart from members of the council) and the first sealing recorded in these minutes was in June of 1934 and thereafter, various

---

opinions on [various] matters before confirming them by the word of the Lord." See *Minutes* 65b.

29 See *Silencing Mormon Polygamy*, Appendixes for the complete affidavit. The relevant language states that John Taylor "placed them under covenant to uphold and sustain the principles of the Gospel, particularly the principle of the Patriarchal Order of Marriage, from thence on as long as they lived. ... He counseled us not to begin our work until told to do so by proper authority."

30 See *Minutes* 8a, 42b. See also *Minutes* 69b for a record of when they discussed the need for a larger meeting hall on April 11, 1935.

31 See *Minutes* 9b.

32 See *Minutes* 10b. By September of 1934, members of the Council of Friends were reporting activities of Church leaders assisting civil authorities in pursuing the arrest of members of that council. Thus, beyond excommunicating polygamists, there were efforts to have them imprisoned as well. *Joseph Lyman Jessop Journal* (9/19/1934).

ordinances were discussed and performed.[33] One entry refers to a decision not to confer the priesthood on anyone without consulting with the council first.[34] Two other entries note that requests for second anointings were considered by the council and granted.[35] Council members thereafter determined: that "widows should not re-marry except under the order of the Priesthood;"[36] that the ordinance of "washing and anointing of expectant mothers" should be considered; that members of the congregation should discontinue kneeling during the administration of the sacrament;[37] that children born to polygamist parents who were not allowed to baptize their children within the structure of the LDS Church could be baptized with the council's sanction and also that a polygamist may properly partake of the sacrament in a private setting when formally disallowed this privilege by the LDS Church;[38] that teachers and deacons were not allowed to administer the sacrament;[39] that Lorin Woolley taught that the priests should "hand the tray to the helps (Teachers, Elders, or others) who, after partaking of it, will pass it to members without reference to positions in the Church;"[40] that homes could be dedicated;[41] and they considered a request for a woman's release from her husband.[42]

The minutes also cover the controversial calling of LeRoy Johnson and Marion Hammon to the council. On

---

33 See *Minutes* 25b.
34 See *Minutes* 39b.
35 See *Minutes* 37b, 55b. See *Abraham* 1:2-4; some authors have interpreted this scripture to suggest that requesting this sacred ordinance is proper. See also John Taylor's discussion of this scripture in *JD* 21: 244-245.
36 See *Minutes* 72b.
37 See *Minutes* 87b. The entry is not clear that the discontinuance of kneeling refers to the members of the congregation but various fundamentalists have informed the author that they believe that this ordinance is most proper when all participants are kneeling but that this non-crucial procedure is not always followed out of convenience.
38 See *Minutes* 89b.
39 See *Minutes* 97b. See *D&C* 20:58.
40 See *Minutes* 6a. The reference to "positions in the Church" is interesting – why, when these members were mostly excommunicated from the Church, would position in the Church matter?
41 See *Minutes* 56b, 58b.
42 See *Minutes* 131b.

April 21, 1941, LeGrand Woolley objected to their callings, testifying that "he felt the call should be confirmed by a personal visit from the other side, as, according to our understanding, has been the case in previous callings." At the next meeting held on April 27, 1941, John Y. Barlow announced that he was "convinced enough of the truthfulness of these callings to take the responsibility, as the senior member of the council."[43] After noting that no one else had received a direct answer to prayers but that no one felt a disposition "to dictate or try to direct those senior" in ordination, Joseph W. Musser "moved, that recognizing John

---

43 Members of the council of friends were supposed to be chosen by Jesus Christ himself. *Items from the Book of Remembrance*, 5. A very emotional and bitter expose written by Jenna Vee Morrison Hammon vividly recalls a discussion between Louis Kelsch and John Y. Barlow concerning these ordinations: "I [Louis Kelsch] asked John Y. Barlow: 'Was this done according to the foolproof plan that God has laid down for calling men into this council? Was this name brought to you by a messenger from the other side?' and John Y. Barlow said, 'No, I called these men. God had nothing to do with it.'" After further questioning, Louis reported: "I went to the door, I opened it, I walked out, and I pulled it real tight, and I have never been back since. ... If they are going to pull things like that on God, on Jesus Christ, on the Holy Ghost, on the priesthood work, and on the priesthood people, I don't want anything to do with it, because it was an utter betrayal of everything, priesthood." Hammon, Jenna Vee Morrison, *The Betrayal of the Godhead, Priesthood Work, and Priesthood People* (self published: 1990), 23.

Later, Hammon claims that Rula Broadbent (J. Leslie Broadbent's wife) and her sister informed Hammon "that John W. Woolley had told Lorin Woolley, when John brought Louis Kelsch's name to Lorin, to be called into the Great High Priesthood Council; 'The name came by appointment from our Father in Heaven and that Louis A. Kelsch would be the last man that God the Eternal Father would call into that Great High Priesthood Council before the setting in order of the house of God took place.'" *See Betrayal,* 25. Spelling and punctuation standardized in all accounts taken from this booklet. See also *Reminiscences* 1:4 (A Discussion with William Thomas); 2:19-21.

This claim is problematic. First, Woolley's 1925 and 1929 statements both claim that the "rights and powers" conferred upon the five "would never be taken from the earth until Christ came." Second, it is well known that Joseph informed the saints that the keys of the kingdom would never be taken from the earth. *D&C* 27:5-13; *Daniel* 2:35-44; *JD* 8:69; Anderson, Devery S. and Bergera, Gary James, editors, *Joseph Smith's Quorum of the Anointed, 1842-1845: A Documentary History,* (Signature Books: 2005), 3-4. See also *D&C* 13. If that is true and if Mormon fundamentalist claims that Lorin C. Woolley held the keys of the kingdom, there is only one way for fundamentalists to reconcile these statements: Lorin C. Woolley gave these keys to someone else to establish a new council of friends. Lastly, the editor has interviewed Mormon fundamentalists who claim to have known Louis Kelsch very well and who claim that he affirmed his support of Joseph Musser's council only a month or two before his death.

as the senior member of our quorum, we accept his recommendation as coming from the Lord, endorse the men named and await further direction from the other side." At the following meeting held on the subject, May 19, 1941, John Y. Barlow expressed his further assurances of these callings, set LeRoy Johnson apart, and requested that Joseph Musser set apart Marion Hammon, which he then did.[44]

---

44 See *Minutes* 146b-48b. Hammon offers this caustic memoir of this controversial calling and ordination: "To see Joseph W. Musser buckle under John Y. Barlow's ungodly demands and turn to be 'his helper' was, to those of us who knew him, a shocking disappointment and we felt cut to the core. The one stalwart, we thought we had, was now gone. Let us remember that it was God who told John W. Woolley and Lorin C. Woolley that it would be John Y. Barlow and his helpers who would get this Great High Priesthood Quorum and Priesthood Work out of order, and lead the people astray." *Betrayal*, 25.
She offers a further hearsay account that John and Lorin Woolley informed Rula and her sister Marian that "every quorum of Great High Priesthood would have its 'Judas' ...[and] that John Y. Barlow was the 'Judas' of that particular council. That he was 'the betrayer' of God, the Godhead, the Priesthood People, and the Priesthood Work. That the only reason that John Y. Barlow was ever called into the Great High Priesthood Council was to get everything out of order from the top to the bottom." *See Id* at 37. See also page 44 where Hammon claims that Carl Jentzsch also testified that he heard these same claims being made by John and Lorin Woolley and that God the Father and Jesus Christ appointed Barlow for this express purpose.
See also Musser's Journal under the date of 11/8/1936 where Joseph Musser records a private conversation wherein he asked John Y. Barlow whether or not "he claimed to hold the keys of priesthood, which he answered in the negative." Note however that statements such as these should be read in context of whether or not Barlow had received the second anointing and/or the second comforter wherein his apostleship would be sealed by the Lord. Musser clearly recognized that John Barlow had been ordained an apostle by Lorin Woolley – there is no question of this fact throughout any of the minutes. The only question that was being asked here was whether or not Barlow claimed to have received his completed second anointing and/or if he had "keys of the priesthood" directly from the Lord that would designate him as the "one man" spoken of in D&C 132:7. It appears, based upon the fact that each member of the council claimed the priesthood of Elijah (bestowed at the time one receives the second anointing), that the question was most likely a simple and direct inquiry as to whether or not John Y. Barlow claimed to have received the second comforter. See *Joseph Lyman Jessop's Journal* (9/20/1934) where he records that "six others have been *called, chosen, and ordained unto this calling* but have not as yet rec'd the confirmation of the Lord himself. It's a peculiar state of wonderment we are in for sure."
Nevertheless, there are a number of fundamentalists who claim to have heard Joseph Musser teach that John Y. Barlow had never received his second anointings so the possibility remains that Musser was asking whether or not Barlow had received his second anointings as of this date. These controversial ordinations and these allegations made by Musser are partially responsible for the ensuing schisms that led to the creation of the AUB and the FLDS

As one might expect from any budding ecclesiastical organization, the council began discussing several other pressing issues brought to them by members of their organization, including whether or not fundamentalist saints should be encouraged to gather[45] and whether or not to make efforts to "set God's House in order" – presumably, by officiating in temple ordinances as a priesthood council rather than relying upon the LDS Church for the ministration of these ordinances.[46] Similarly, they discussed that their efforts should not "draw away from the Church, but rather to strengthen the hands of the Priesthood."[47]

Members of the council were also concerned as to whether or not it was their position to proselyte. Initially, this council felt an obligation to conduct missionary work. Joseph Musser felt so strongly about it that in a prayer circle, he "pledged our own blood and lives if necessary to help redeem the Saints and reinstate them before the Lord."[48] However, rather than send missionaries door to door, they decided to let their publications "do that work at present."[49] Indeed, financial records of this initial council indicate a very heavy emphasis was placed on spreading the gospel – on average, one third to one half of all of their donations were spent on publications outlining their basic doctrinal beliefs and claims to the priesthood[50] and they made conscientious efforts to distribute literature to leaders of other churches and

---

organizations. Many fundamentalists also became independents as a result of the ensuing "split."

45 The council initially decided that their duty was to keep the spirit and not colonize (*See Minutes* 95b, 110b) but they later decide to encourage saints in New York to gather (*See Minutes* 141b, 142b).

46 *See Minutes* 105b. There were concurrent rumors that the temple garment was going to be changed. See also *Minutes* 83b.

47 *See Minutes* 67b.

48 *See Minutes* 64b. Elsewhere, Musser wrote that upon this Grand Council "rested the responsibility of bearing the gospel message to the world – their testimony being immediately in force upon all the world – with power to rend the kingdoms of the world, which power pertains only to this order of the priesthood, and not primarily to appendage callings." *Supplement to the New and Everlasting Covenant of Marriage*, 103.

49 See *Minutes* 31b.

50 *See Minutes* 98b; 104b; unnumbered pages between 106b and 107b; 117b and 118b; 132b and 133b; 145b and 146b.

to state officials so that they "might be made acquainted with our position."[51]

They also discussed non-priesthood issues such as: whether the so called "White Horse" prophecy was authentic enough to republish;[52] the status of free masonry as the "Mammon of Unrighteousness;"[53] the alleged declaration that Satan is the god of masonry in the higher degrees;[54] and whether or not it would be appropriate to have group round dances.[55]

For one acquainted with the history of fundamentalist Mormonism, the record of the final meetings in these minutes unveil the subtle brewings of dissention that ultimately led to "the split" between what later became known as the FLDS and the AUB.[56] These references tend to be sketchy but they clearly delineate disputes over authority and stewardship within the Short Creek colony.[57]

In addition to these disputes, dispute over authority within the council began to erupt as well. Unfortunately, the strikingly abrupt manner in which the minutes end leave multiple questions of succession unanswered. The minutes do inform us that the senior member of the council

---

51 See *Minutes* 131b, 77b. They also prayed "for an understanding with the leaders of the Church [t]hat we might be able to reason together." *See* 68b.
52 See *Minutes* 124b. They decided that it was not "considered authentic enough to republish without more detailed information."
53 Nineteenth century Mormons also engaged in this discussion. Heber C. Kimball referred to masonry as the "degenerated" priesthood and others echoed this teaching. See *Joseph's Quorum of Anointed*, xxii, 9, 19, 46.
54 See *Minutes* 9a, 127b.
55 *See Minutes* 60b, 137b.
56 FLDS stands for the Fundamentalist Church of Jesus Christ of Latter-day Saints. While generally quiet and isolated from society at large, this group has garnished national attention twice because of government raids and legal efforts to prohibit their practices of plural marriage and marriages to underage girls. AUB stands for the Apostolic United Brethren. In comparison, the AUB has managed to keep out of the national media spotlight for the most part. Although acknowledged by government officials as generally law abiding and open to communication with legal authorities, the general public often confuses the AUB with the FLDS. While both of these groups find their roots with the 1886 ordinations, the FLDS has apparently abandoned its council for a leadership headed by the "one man." The majority of fundamentalist Mormon groups stem from these two organizations.
57 See *Minutes* 86b, 95b.

presides.[58] Additionally, they inform us that Lorin C. Woolley specifically designated J. Leslie Broadbent as his successor through revelatory means.[59] Because J. Leslie Broadbent was the next senior in ordination and because he had been designated by Lorin C. Woolley as his successor, the question of succession was not challenged during Broadbent's short tenure.

Nevertheless, as alluded to earlier, "presiding" and being designated as "the one man" were not considered synonymous by members of the council during John Y. Barlow's administration. Accordingly, when Joseph W. Musser questioned John Y. Barlow as to whether or not he "held the keys" in November of 1936 (while John Y. Barlow was presiding over the council),[60] John Y. Barlow showed no offense to the question and freely answered in the negative. Then, two years later, Joseph W. Musser admitted in a council meeting that, as of December 19, 1938, no member of that quorum was a fully qualified apostle.[61] The minutes specifically note that no one present at that meeting held any ill feelings towards any other member of the council so it does not appear that this statement should be read as a challenge to John Y. Barlow's status as the presiding member of the quorum.[62]

Nevertheless, differences as to whether or not the presiding member of the council of friends could designate a successor who was not the next senior member of that council (by order of ordination) is what ultimately led to the famous "split." The minutes themselves do not resolve this question conclusively. Despite the disappointingly abrupt ending of the minutes, this historical record remains monumentally important to members of the AUB, FLDS, Centennial Park, and Kingston groups and it is of monumental importance to the large but unorganized mass of

---

58 See *Minutes* 95b .

59 See *Minutes* 1a.

60 See *Musser's Journal*, 11/8/1936.

61 See *Minutes* 115b.

62 The reader should note however that John Y. Barlow was not present at this meeting.

independent Mormon fundamentalists that claim their priesthood authority from the Lorin C. Woolley line. Given the vast pool of folklore and conflicting claims associated with questions of priesthood authority and the scope of authority held by these various groups, this volume will undoubtedly prove to be an invaluable resource to these various latter-day saints.

Brief History[1] of Meetings and Teachings Pertaining to

The School of the Prophets

and to the Special Calling in the Patriarchal Order of the Priesthood

September 1, 1932 to January 11, 1934

From statements made by Lorin C. Woolley, it is assumed he was ordained to the Patriarchal Order of the Priesthood[2] in 1882, and in 1886, the personnel of the Council stood as follows:

John Taylor
John W. Woolley
Lorin C. Woolley
Joseph F. Smith
Wilford Woodruff
Charles H. Wilcken[3]
John Smith (Patriarch of Church)

---

1 The reader should note that these initial pages are a summary of School of the Prophet meetings that occurred before January 11, 1934 - these were taken from Joseph Musser's journals and therefore should not be considered official minutes.

2 *Minutes* 8a tells us that this "Patriarchal Order" refers to the Apostleship. However, the reader should note that in *Minutes* 4a, this same terminology is used to refer to the keys held by the presiding patriarch of the Church of Jesus Christ of Latter-day Saints.

3 The absence of George Q. Cannon and Samuel Bateman from this list should be noted. In addition to this detail (and the subsequent replacement of Wilford W. Woodruff with Lorenzo Snow), other sources suggest that the status of members of this council were not static - much like the first presidency of the LDS church. See Briney, Drew, *Silencing Mormon Polygamy: Failed Persecutions, Divided Saints, and the Rise of Mormon Fundamentalism*, (Hindsight Publications: 2009), 325 fn 57.

Upon the withdrawal of Wilford Woodruff, in consequence of signing the Manifesto, Lorenzo Snow was added.

Membership in the Council steadily decreased through deaths until after the death of John W. Woolley, December 13, 1928 Lorin C. Woolley was left the lone member thereof.

J. Leslie Broadbent and John Y. Barlow, who had been designated as members by revelation through John W. Woolley before his death, were set apart on March 6, 1929 in the order named. Joseph W. Musser was set apart May 14, 1929; Charles F. Zitting and LeGrand Woolley (in the order named), were set apart on July 22, 1932; and Louis A. Kelsch on January 26, 1933.

The Council now (January 1934) consists of:

Lorin C. Woolley[4]
J. Leslie Broadbent[5]
John Y. Barlow
Joseph W. Musser
Charles F. Zitting
LeGrand Woolley
Louis A. Kelsch

Instructions were given from time to time, while the Council membership was being completed, by Lorin C. Woolley, until regular meetings were begun. The first regular meeting was held at the home of Brother Broadbent, Thursday, September 1, 1932. These meetings, designated as the "School of the Prophets," were held with but few interruptions on Thursday or (sometimes) on Friday of each week, either at the home of J. Leslie Broadbent (1449 East 17th South), the office of Joseph W. Musser (302 Vermont Building), or at 744 East South Temple Street, all in Salt Lake City, Utah.

---

4 See *Minutes* 41b: Lorin C. Woolley died on September 19, 1934.
5 See *Minutes* 67b: J. Leslie Broadbent died on March 21, 1935.

At these meetings, save at the first few, the Sacrament was administered, using unleavened bread and wine, both furnished by Brother Broadbent. The brethren took turns in conducting the exercises according to their seniority in ordination.[6]

In August 1933, the ordinance of feet washing was taught by Lorin C. Woolley, and was begun to be administered, J. Leslie Broadbent, leading; he performing the ordinance for each member, Joseph W. Musser performing for him. This procedure continued from week to week when a full quorum of seven could be present, the next in seniority officiating, and Brother Musser taking care of the ordinance for the officiator. This ordinance was completed on November 22, 1933, by Lorin C. Woolley officiating. In his blessing of Brother Broadbent, Brother Woolley designated him, through revelation, (as he explained afterwards) as the one holding the keys to revelation jointly with himself, in the same manner as they had first been held jointly by Joseph Smith and Oliver Cowdery, the first and second Elders. See D&C 20:2-3 and 124:94-96.

2 A

This sacred ordinance (feet washing) being completed, the brethren all felt to rejoice and praise the Lord for His wondrous blessings. They felt a complete fellowship with each other, with a love that only God could inspire; and now that this sacred ordinance had been completed, each of the brethren officiating in their turn, they should go forward, in abiding faith, wrestling with the Lord for the Confirmation of the Second Comforter, in order to be fully endowed with

---

6 This detail is what makes breaking the original coded minutes possible. Nevertheless, there are enough exceptions to this purported rule that breaking the code was not simply mathematical in nature.

power and authority to properly discharge their duties in the sacred calling to which they had been ordained.

It is most regrettable that with the completion of the ordinance of feet washing, Brother Woolley took sick and has not been able to meet with the Council since. Meanwhile the responsibility of leadership is being borne off by Brother Broadbent in a manner that fully testifies to his being richly endowed with the spirit and gift of leadership.

Items of information have come from the mouth of Lorin C. Woolley from time to time, of which the following may be termed a brief summary:[7]

At the Carlisle home in 1886,[8] President John Taylor stated to Lorin C. Woolley that Joseph Smith, as a resurrected being,[9] guided Brigham Young across the plains and led him to Utah. His remains were not brought to Utah by wagon as many have supposed.

An officer in the Church, not living the Patriarchal law, cannot legally sit in judgment on a case of one who is living such a law.

The young people of today who have not had the fullness of the Gospel preached to them are not among those who will apostatize as one cannot apostatize from a principle which he has not been taught and which he has not received.

Many taking plural wives and failing to live this principle; their wives will be taken from them and given to others who are worthy – among them, men who would have lived the

---

7 Virtually all of the following materials have been previously published in *Joseph Musser's Book of Remembrance*. However, *Joseph W. Musser's Book of Remembrance* is much larger and contains more of Lorin C. Woolley's teachings than those contained within these summarized minutes.

8 This is most likely not a reference to the famous September 26/27, 1886 events. See *Silencing Mormon Polygamy*, 119.

9 For information on Joseph Smith's resurrection, see *Silencing Mormon Polygamy*, 119-120 and 130 fn 14.

principle but could not because of physical or other handicaps.

"Thus saith the Lord God of Israel to my servants the Presidency and Quorum of the Twelve: I am not pleased with your work." Gist of revelation said to have been received by Apostle Orson F. Whitney shortly before his death, and rejected by President Heber J. Grant.

"Holy Spirit of Promise": Proceeding from the Holy Ghost, sealing with promise, such as those accepting Patriarchal Marriage.

Peleg was a great and mighty Prophet who, with his people, was taken from the earth as was Enoch.[10] Those like Peleg and Enoch, who are translated, ascend away from the earth. The earth descended away from Kolob when the fall took place. Some day this earth will return to meet the parts that have been taken from it and which are more righteous. Then the earth will again be perfect and be crowned with its paradisiacal glory.

Celestial Glory, compared with the sun. As at break of day the sun appears mild and grows brighter and more intense each minute until noonday so shines the different degrees of glory in the Celestial Kingdom.

Man must enter all kingdoms of glory, Celestial, Terrestrial or Telestial, by baptism and the accompanying ordinances. Until he accepts such, he must remain in a kingdom without a glory.

---

10 See Briney, Drew, *Understanding Adam God Teachings: A Comprehensive Resource of Adam-God Materials*, (Self Published: 2005), 263ff. Within that section, note specifically the *Journal of Samuel Holister Rogers*, 17; *MS* 1:258; and the *Journal of Wandle Mace*, 38-39, 48 entries where Peleg is specifically mentioned in connection with parts of the earth that were taken.

3 A ᏣᏰ

"I ordain you to become a Patriarch when you have complied with the requirements." Language used by Joseph F. Smith on the head of Hyrum G. Smith.

The section near Lee's Ferry in Arizona is the hub of this intermountain country between Yucatan City and Canada.[11] It was set apart under the direction of Brigham Young by John W. Woolley for the gathering of the Saints. It is a choice land. One acre there will prove as productive as five acres here. One well will develop enough water for a thousand acres. Here is one place water will spring up in the desert as spoken of by Isaiah.[12] Prayer circles of the Priesthood will be scattered from Mexico, through that section to Canada, to keep the Asiatics and Europeans from overrunning this country.

Adam probably had three wives on earth before Mary the mother of Jesus. Eve, meaning first:[13] Phoebe,[14] meaning second; and Sarah, meaning third.[15] Sarah was probably the mother of Seth.[16]

Joseph of Armenia, proxy husband of Mary, had one wife before Mary and four additional after. John the Revelator was a son of Mary by Joseph.

Shem and Melchizedek are one and the same. Melchizedek meaning "Great High priest."

---

11 The Grand Canyon officially begins at Lee's Ferry, which is located on the Colorado river in northern Arizona. It is in the middle of Glenn, Marble, and Paria Canyons and was settled by Mormon pioneer John D. Lee.

12 There are three possible scriptures that Woolley may have been referring to: *Isaiah* 35:6; 43:20; and 48:21. See also *D&C* 133:29.

13 In Hebrew, Eve means first woman or mother of all living.

14 There is no Phebe or Phoebe in the Old Testament. In Greek, Phebe/Phoebe means bright or radiant.

15 In Hebrew, Sarai/Sarah means princess or noble woman.

16 cf. *Genesis* 5:3.

Seth began the building of the Pyramid and Shem (Melchizedek) finished it. If the measurements could be made with absolute accuracy, one could tell the day and hour the Savior will come.

Peleg took with him a greater amount of earth than either Enoch or the "Lost Tribes." He was the greatest Prophet in the Adamic dispensation.

Joseph Smith was called "Gazalem," or one who gazes (a seer) also Baurak Ale, both Adamic terms and which pertain to his respective callings. At a meeting here since his resurrection, Joseph Smith repeated the statement, "Would to God I could tell you who I am."[17] The Saints are not yet prepared to know their Prophet leader.[18]

Joseph Smith is probably a literal descendent of Jesus Christ (of Jewish and Ephraimic lineage), the blood of Judah probably predominating, which is the ruling power.

The last revelation received by Joseph Smith was while in Carthage jail, written by John Taylor, which, in part, Lorin C. Woolley was permitted to see.

John the Revelator is working especially for the salvation of the people on the European continent, while the three Nephite Apostles are assigned to this continent. These apostles may be assigned from time to time to conduct mortal agents of God from place to place when special work by such agents is necessary, such as setting Lamanites apart to special work, holding Grand Council meetings, etc.

---

[17] The original statement follows: "Would to God, brethren, I could tell you who I am! Would to God I could tell you what I know! But you would call it blasphemy, and there are men upon this stand who would want to take my life." Whitney, Orson F., *Life of Heber C. Kimball*, 322-23 (as recounted by Heber C. Kimball).
[18] See *Minutes* 5a where Lorin C. Woolley taught that Joseph Smith was one of the gods.

President John Taylor could not be taken by death until Joseph F. Smith could get home from Honolulu to receive instructions necessary for the continuance of the work.[19]

Six have held the Keys to the Kingdom in this dispensation:
Joseph Smith
Brigham Young
John Taylor
Wilford Woodruff
John W. Woolley[20] and now
Lorin C. Woolley.

4 A ☙

Six have held the Keys to the Presidency of the Church:
Joseph Smith
Brigham Young
John Taylor
Wilford Woodruff
Lorenzo Snow and
Joseph F. Smith.
They never passed to Heber J. Grant.

---

19 See *Silencing Mormon Polygamy*, 201-03, fn 49.

20 It is interesting to note that this list skips Lorenzo Snow and Joseph F. Smith. In an undated affidavit referring to 1914 events, John W. Woolley states that he felt that he was authorized by Joseph F. Smith to perform plural marriages at that time – a detail that suggests he believed that Joseph F. Smith held the sealing keys in 1914. See *Silencing Mormon Polygamy,* 181-82 (cf. also Daniel Bateman's 1934 Affidavit in the Appendices wherein he states that Woolley was not to exercise his priesthood until told to do so by "proper authority."). Although Lorin C. Woolley's terminology is not identical to that used in the nineteenth century, one could reasonably extrapolate that the sealing keys were associated with the keys of the kingdom or the keys of the patriarchal order. See *Silencing Mormon Polygamy*, chapter 12. Nevertheless, Joseph F. Smith is not listed as the holder of either of these keys.
It is also interesting to notice that Lorin C. Woolley claims that the keys of the kingdom passed from Wilford Woodruff to John W. Woolley. He claimed that this was due to Woodruff's 1890 manifesto. See *Truth* 6:21-22; 8:262; 9:142, 144, 251; 10:329-30; and 16:79; see also *Sermons of Joseph W. Musser*, 52, 79; *LeRoy S. Johnson Sermons* 1:211; and *Testimony of Moroni Jessop*, 14. He also claimed that these keys passed "in natural order." That is, they passed based upon seniority in that quorum. See *Truth* 9:74.

Six have held the Keys to the Patriarchal order:[21]
Joseph Smith
Hyrum Smith
"Uncle" John Smith
John Smith
John W. Woolley and
Lorin C. Woolley.

We are now in the seventh cycle of years.

Joseph Smith had predicted that a member of the Quorum of Apostles would occupy a seat in the United States Senate. This was thought impossible by Judge Douglas and others. Reed Smoot's election to the Senate was the means of fulfilling that prophecy.

Butter (as spoken of in Isaiah 7:15) means whole, rich milk, while honey is native unadulterated sweets. The two of them are natural foods.

The largest faction of the Church membership will always be with Joseph Smith and his assistants, and therefore the Gospel will never be taken from the earth or given to another people.[22]

The Grand Council of the Kingdom has been attended by such men as Bonaparte, Gladstone and Disraeli in order to get their views and purposes of Government and the reasons for doing certain things. These men had as their ideal the attainment of the Kingdom of God on earth. Lennon, Trotsky and others had and have like motives, but lack the knowledge and ability to accomplish it. Theodore Roosevelt

---

21 Cross-referencing statements in *Minutes* 2a and 8a suggests that the "Patriarchal Order" refers to the Apostleship. However, here, the definition of "Patriarchal Order" clearly refers to the keys of the presiding patriarch.
22 See *3 Nephi* 16:10-15; 21:12-24; 22:3.

was a member of the Grand Council and accepted the Patriarchal order of marriage. He was given his endowments.

The Temple at Jackson County will be built after the great war.[23]

A Lamanite Prophet is laboring among the Lamanites in Yucatan; has been laboring about eight months (January 1931).[24]

The three Nephites are laboring among the Lamanites of South and Central American and in Mexico.

There are about two million Indians in Yucatan and about eleven million Lamanites in Mexico
and Central America.

When the Lamanites commence to receive the Gospel, we will witness a nation being born in a day, as spoken of by the Prophet.[25]

Christ was the first fruits of the resurrection; also an ensample for all time. He received from the grave (tomb) the identical body he had in moral life and which was crucified. So will all men receive their real bodies in the resurrection, but in perfect form, and all bodies will be, or grow to be, the full stature of the spirit.[26]

"He that blasphemeth against me or those whom I have anointed, shall come under condemnation and will be

---

23 *Minutes* 12a informs us that Lorin C. Woolley expected the temple to be ready for ordinance work before the fall of 1936.

24 Some fundamentalists believe that this Lamanite prophet holds all of the keys of the priesthood held by man on earth (See *D&C* 132:7). If this position were true, the minutes of Lorin C. Woolley's school of the prophets must be rejected because they claim (explicitly and implicitly) that J. Leslie Broadbent held all of the keys that Lorin C. Woolley held.

25 *Isaiah* 66:8. cf. *Minutes* 8a, 10a.

26 This suggests that Lorin C. Woolley rejected the doctrine (taught by Joseph E. Taylor and others) wherein children are said to be resurrected at the age they died and wherein they are said to stay that age throughout all eternity.

damned." Jesus Christ to Joseph Smith after personally anointing him in the spring of 1831.[27]

Some wives of Jesus Christ: Martha, Mary, Phoebe, Sarah, Rebecca, Josephine,[28] Mary Magdalene.

To be the head of a dispensation, seven wives necessary. Five wives necessary in the holding of the Keys to the Kingdom or of the Church or to the Patriarchal Order.[29]

5 A ☙

Two Jewish brethren have been translated in our day and are now working among the Jews. This happened recently (spoken May 12, 1932), one within a year ago. Members of the Grand Council of the Kingdom of God.

In the Lee's Ferry section of Arizona is the principle place where Jesus met the Nephite people after His resurrection.

---

27 Which anointing Lorin C. Woolley is referring to is unclear. In what may or may not be related, historian, D. Michael Quinn strongly argues that the restoration of the Melchizedek priesthood was restored sometime around 1831-32 - not in 1929 as official LDS Church history has portrayed. See *Origins*, 14-26, especially page 26. There is no official record indicating when the Melchizedek priesthood was restored.

28 This doctrine is taught more fully in the eighth number and fourteenth volume of *Truth* magazine. If the names of Phoebe, Sarah, Rebecca, and Josephine originate from a publication, the source is unclear. However, *Minutes* 3a informs us that Lorin C. Woolley taught that Phoebe means "second" and Sarah means "third" so there is some possibility that he was referring to these names as offices.

29 This teaching of course implies that John W. Woolley, Lorin C. Woolley, Lorenzo Snow (8 in Nauvoo), Hyrum Smith (4 in Nauvoo), and John Smith (7 in Nauvoo) all had five wives at the time they held their respective priesthood positions. cf. Smith, George D., *Nauvoo Polygamy: But We Called it Celestial Marriage*, (Signature Books: 2008), 312-14. Of the nineteenth century leadership listed, only Hyrum Smith does not meet the criterion established by Lorin C. Woolley. Whether or not John W. Woolley and/or Lorin C. Woolley were plurally married and/or how many wives they each had is a matter of dispute among fundamentalist Mormons and their detractors.

Shortly before being murdered, Joseph Smith said, "I am going to take my place in the Heavens," until which time, John Taylor claims not to have had a clear understanding of who Joseph Smith was, ONE OF THE GODS.[30]

Not that which you have, but that "which you seemeth to have,"[31] shall be taken away from you and given to him that hath; meaning the wife or wives whom he is unworthy of.

He that will not provide for his loved ones, is worse than an infidel,[32] carries a special meaning: that provision has reference to embracing the fullness of marriage, else the family organization is not complete and happiness cannot result.

Temple work done by unmarried people is only effective as they complete the marriage relation, as the man is not without the woman, nor the woman without the man in the Lord. Those who have not taken their wives through the veil will have the privilege of doing so, if faithful.

"And it shall come to pass that the noble of my spirits shall be preserved to come forth in the last days to fight the fight."[33]

"Oh, ye of little understanding, how oft would I have taught you, but you could not receive it."[34]

An Elect person is one whose anointings and blessings are such as to enable him to resist the temptations of Satan.[35]

---

30 There are several teachings of the prophet Joseph Smith that have been construed to mean that Joseph Smith believed that he was the Holy Ghost before his probation. The most famous of these statements merely alludes to such a possibility: "Joseph also said that the Holy Ghost is now in a state of Probation which if he should perform in righteousness he may pass through the same or a similar course of things that the Son has." *WJS*, 245. See also *JD* 4:270.

31 See *Luke* 8:18.

32 See *1 Timothy* 5:8.

33 cf. *Abraham* 3:22-23.

34 cf. *Matthew* 23:37; *Mark* 13:34;

35 cf. *D&C* 29:7; 33:6; 35:21; 84:34.

The Zion spoken of, to which the righteous would flee for safety and where their money will be safe, is the region occupied by the Saints in the Rocky Mountains, according to instructions from Joseph Smith, Brigham Young, John Taylor, etc.

Those who are living the law and who are engaged in setting the Church in order, from now on will not have to shed blood. The wicked among the Mormons, as in the world, will slay the wicked.

"I would rather be a door keeper in the Kingdom of God, than President of the Church." John Taylor.

President Taylor said on different occasions, that these mountains (the Wasatch range) are full of gold and when it is needed the Lord will bring it forth.

Brigham Young stated in substance: The Gentiles will open up the mines, which will later be closed, after which the Lord will direct the Saints to reopen them, take the treasure out to be used in building up Zion.

Those who charge the Saints usury will lose what they have as well as what they seem to have, and they will go to hell cross-lots.

6 A

James and John the lesser, were sons of Joseph of Armenia by his first wife, Mary being his second wife. John the Revelator, Sam and Isaac, were sons of Joseph by Mary, Mother of Christ. John the Revelator took the wives of Jesus after the crucifixion.

John the Revelator, under the direction of Jesus Christ, taught Joseph Smith the pattern of the garment of the Priesthood. He cut out a pattern and then had Joseph Smith do likewise. The collar is the crown of the Priesthood.[36] Those discarding garments, after having worn them, cannot again wear them unless authorized to do so by proper authority. Garments may be rolled up on legs and arms, to avoid dirt, when occupied in such work, and to avoid the gaze of wicked people. "What's dirtier than the gaze of the Wicked?"

John the Revelator held the Keys of the Patriarchal order from his father, Joseph, and those given special work in connection with this Patriarchal calling, and who remain true and faithful, are generally of that lineage.

The word "fasting" comes from "kaluka," Adamic, and means prayer or praying as expressed in the Hebrew, or feasting. Jesus fasted for forty days and nights but did partake of food to sustain his body. In other words he was praying and communing with his Father forty days and nights, after which he was left to be tried of the devil. Joseph Smith got much of his great knowledge through such fasting or prayer, which would last for a week at a time, but he partook of food sparingly during the time, as did Jesus during his fasting or prayer.

President Joseph F. Smith claimed it was revealed to him by mouth of his Uncle Joseph Smith, the Prophet, that the offices in the Priesthood, such as deacon, teacher, priest, elder, seventy, etc. were but appendages to the Priesthood and that the Priesthood itself must be conferred before the office is given. Hence the present plan to ordain a man to the office merely, is in error. President John Taylor learning from President Smith of this revelation, said, "Of course that

---

36 This and other teachings of the symbolisms of the original garment are found in the 1932 affidavit. See *Truth* 2:35.

is the proper order," i.e. to confer the Priesthood before the office.[37]

Joseph Smith walked over the Mississippi river, on the water, from Nauvoo to Montrose, after his boat had capsized, the brethren with him being instructed to remain and procure another boat, he going ahead to fill an appointment, so says Grandpa Edwin D. Woolley and Samuel W. Richards.

Shem is being preached to by men set apart for that purpose under direction of President Joseph F. Smith, educated Chinese, Russians, etc. They are preaching the doctrine of the Kingdom, and not establishing the Church. In fact, all nations are being preached to.

Sacrament should be administered by Priests assisted, when necessary, by Teachers (not Deacons). Priests should pronounce the blessing, partake as Jesus did, then hand the tray to the helps (Teachers, Elders, or others) who, after partaking of it, will pass it to members without reference to positions in the Church.

Brethren holding the Priesthood and deprived of the privilege of partaking of the sacrament in their wards, may administer it at home.

Bishops, as Bishops, can only preside over the Aaronic Priesthood. They preside over ward members as High Priests.

7A

Judas was the cousin of Jesus and the only apostle who was sufficiently blessed with light and knowledge, to enable him to commit the unpardonable sin and become a Son of

[37] See *Silencing Mormon Polygamy*, 222-23, fn. 8.

Perdition, until after the resurrection of Christ, when the Holy Ghost became a witness.

So long as there are a few people in the Church who are living the fullness of the Gospel, or the Patriarchal order of marriage, God will acknowledge His Church.

To have sufficient knowledge to commit the unpardonable sin, one must be anointed by the Savior himself, after which, to deny Him, "shall not be forgiven in this world, nor in the world to come."[38]

If a good woman eligible for marriage, chooses a good man and expresses the wish to be married to him, he is bound to receive her unless barred from such act through physical disabilities or financial distress, in which event, however, she may still chose him, she assuming the consequences. Should he refuse and cause her to sin unto destruction, he will be responsible for her fall and must redeem her in eternity.

A father living the Patriarchal order, must be consulted before his daughter can be married to a man, and her father's consent be obtained.

President Taylor said Paul was married and had several wives.

Priesthood gives authority, but it takes the appointment to properly exercise that authority.[39]

Keys to the Patriarchal order of the Priesthood, are not necessarily held by the presiding Patriarch of the Church.

---

38 See *Matthew* 12:32.

39 This is a very important teaching to understand when reading these minutes. See *Minutes* 115b. Although the council clearly believed that they had been given the authority to act in their individual and joint capacities, they continued to pray for a confirmation of their appointment from the heavens for many months.

David is still in hell, but is there preaching the Gospel and rejoicing in his blessings.[40] He will have wives given unto him by the Lord.

The Church and its members came under condemnation in voting to sustain President Grant's statement in April 1931 conference, to the extent that they did it understandingly. Those who are in their right minds and who have been taught the law and who have read the law, and who voted to sustain President Grant, will come under condemnation.

Franklin D. Roosevelt is much like his cousin Theodore, was. He believes in religious liberty; and those who live the Patriarchal order of marriage as a religious right, he claims cannot be interfered with under the constitution. He has been consulted and has promised to do the right thing, if elected.

Theodore Roosevelt's split with Taft was over matters pertaining to the Mormon Church and the Kingdom of God.

Lincoln forfeited his right to the blessings of the Lord by signing the Cullom bill against polygamy and threatening to destroy the other "twin relic of barbarism," polygamy, as he put it, when he got through with the slave question. He broke his covenants which were very sacred and specific. Other Presidents, such as Taft, Wilson, Hoover and Curtis have broken their covenants.

8 A

Brigham Young said Lincoln would not live to carry out his threat against the Mormons, and he didn't.

Reed Smoot has been tried in the balance and found wanting.

---

40 See *Psalms* 16:10.

Instructions to the five, September 27, 1886:

"You will have the weight of this world upon you, and one of you will have to stand alone. Joseph Smith laid his hands upon the heads while John Taylor set them apart, or acted as mouth. Joseph Smith expressed surprise that George Q. Cannon did not know that Lorin C. Woolley had been an Apostle for several years.[41]

The Jews in Russia are seeking to establish the Order of Enoch but are starting wrong. When the Gospel of the Kingdom is preached in its fullness the Russian Jews will accept it and a nation will be born in a day.[42]

The flag of the United States was as much the result of the inspiration as was the constitution. It is the flag of the Kingdom of God; the blue field meaning "God's Kingdom;" the stripes, "Purity of Government and the shedding of blood if necessary;" the stars representing the nations coming in under the flag.

Melchizedek and Shem are the same person – King of Salem. He went up as Enoch.[43] Had many wives like Solomon. The Chinese are of Shem, as are the Mormons, but by a different mother.

Russia will likely fight for the rights of the Jews, and the bear will put its paw on the lion.[44] Jewish money will make the war possible and will be controlled by the Priesthood. Jews are friends, Catholics are enemies.

Hyrum Smith had been set apart by Joseph to succeed him the Presidency of the Church, and Brigham had been

41 The opening statements of these summarized minutes inform us that Lorin C. Woolley claimed to have been ordained to the patriarchal order in 1882.
42 cf. *Minutes* 4a, 10a.
43 cf. *Minutes* 3a.
44 See *Juvenile Instructor* 25:162 cf. *Daniel* 7 and *Revelation* 13.

promised that he would some time come to the Presidency.[45] When Hyrum, through his death, failed to become President, Joseph's mantle fell upon Brigham, who looked, talked and acted like Joseph.

Each President of the Church has designated his successor, before death, and passed on the Keys of the Presidency of the Church, except in the case of Heber J. Grant, whom Joseph F. Smith designated but did not confer the keys, he taking them with him.[46]

"I am going into the heavens to take my place," remarked Joseph Smith, a few days before his martyrdom. "I am rolling the burden off onto you brethren, but I will assist you."[47]

There are more of the valiant spirits reserved to come forth in this day, than came anciently, because the work now calls for more strength and power. It is likely that the faithful will not wait long after death before obtaining their resurrection, and when they will begin in the preparation to create worlds for their children.

Two homes have been dedicated for a place where Jesus can come and abide and bring with him his wives or friends; Home of Lorin C. Woolley so dedicated by John Taylor, and the home of J. Leslie Broadbent, dedicated by Lorin C. Woolley.

---

[45] For Brigham Young's promise and a memoir of his designation, see Andrus, Hyrum L., *They Knew the Prophet,* (Deseret Book: 1979), 38; and *MS* 4:101. For circumstantial evidence that Joseph intended Hyrum Smith to succeed him, see *HC* 3:41-42 (Hyrum Smith is listed as the "Vice-President" of the Church); *HC* 6:41 (Hyrum Smith and Joseph Smith both signed and published Elder George J. Adams' appointment to a mission to Russia in the Times and Seasons as "Presidents of the Church of Jesus Christ of Latter-day Saints." The footnote to this entry notes that the "fact that Sidney Rigdon and William Law did not sign this document as in the First Presidency should be noted."); *RLDSCH* 2:107; *HC* 2:509; *MS* 16:56-57; *Silencing Mormon Polygamy*, 261-262, 284-85, 299-300, 320. cf. *Minutes* 10a.

[46] cf. *Minutes* 11a.

[47] It sounds like this could be referring to Joseph's March, 1844 "Last Charge" but the suggestion that this happened "a few days before his martyrdom" may indicate otherwise.

Jesus glorified the Father by raising children to His name.

Mountains have been raised up on earth's surface at various places, to hide and protect sacred places from desecration; and the time will come when, through [continued next page]

9 A

Faith and the power of the Priesthood, they will be removed by God's servants whose right it is to possess or occupy such places. Mount Tabby in the Uintah Basin, was seen, in vision, to be thus removed.

Kingdom of God was organized in the winter of 1843-1844 by Joseph Smith, when the Grand Council was fully completed.

Jews of Palestine and the Mohammedans are uniting against England. The latter of Hagar and the former of Sarah. Mohammed was a Prophet of God, but not the person his followers consider him to be. Three Jews now laboring under the Kingdom of God in Jerusalem among the Jews and the Mohammedans, named: Wickersham, Rosenbaum and Izenstein.

Unless we return the Philippines, Japan will take them from us, thereby causing great embarrassment to us. She will take them in any event. Morrow resigned to allow J. Reuben Clark to become Ambassador to Mexico, and Clark has been keeping Japan back from invading through Mexico.

Shortly before the Manifesto was issued Wilford Woodruff was shown, in vision, two courses:[48]

---

[48] See *Deseret Weekly* 11/14/1891.

First – To stand for the law and let the Gentiles and Government confiscate both Church and individual property, leaving the battle for the Lord to fight;

Second – Issue the Manifesto, hold on to the property, but open the way for whoredom and destruction among the people, the result of rejecting the perfect law of social conduct. He was prevailed upon to choose the latter course.

Special brethren have been appointed and set apart to receive revelations and special direction on specified subjects, which revelations, after being approved by the mouthpiece of God, are made official. Thus Wilford Woodruff, by appointment, received the revelation of 1880, his special mission being to get the word of the Lord with reference to our enemies and the course to be pursued to thwart their evil designs. Lorenzo Snow's mission was pertaining to the finances of the Church, tithing, etc. Joseph F. Smith and others had other special callings.

"Regarding my servants whom I have called to this labor: Men shall speak evilly and do all manner of things against you and those who seek to serve me, but if you continue faithful to the covenants that you have made with me, it will be to their shame and to your triumph."

Covenants: "Life, property, wives, children, friends, and all that God has given me are on the altar."

Mammon of Unrighteousness: Those who are not of you, but who are bound together with an oath to uphold the inalienable rights of men, Free Masons.

"Friends" in the Priesthood have original jurisdiction, their authority coming direct from God. Others receiving the Priesthood receive it from the "Friends" and it is a delegated power.

All male members, above the calling of an Elder, must live the Patriarchal law to qualify them for their callings, otherwise their Priesthood may be called into question by the "Friends." To teach the fullness of the Gospel as a Seventy is to do, he must first live the Gospel.

Children dying before reaching the age of accountability are subjects of the Kingdom of God, those not born under the covenant becoming servants to the faithful, while those born under the covenant may become a part of their parent's Kingdom and raise up seed for the glorification thereof; but can never [continued next page]

10 A ☙

become Gods in their own right, as is also true of those Latter-day Saints who fail in mortality to live the fullness of the Gospel. They may, through vicarious work, be permitted to help their parents who were faithful. Our status before we came here determines, in large measure, our final exaltation.

The 144,000 are to be Gods. They were true in spirit and will remain true here.

Wine purchased from the enemy at Kirtland for Sacramental purposes was poisoned; hence, people were permitted to use water until they could make wine that was pure. Unfermented juices are not wine as spoken of by the Savior.

Abraham was required to offer up Isaac as an atonement for the sin of permitting Sarah to cast Hagar out after the latter becoming Abraham's wife.[49] Abraham, Isaac, and Sarah all understood the matter. By consenting to it, Isaac became the heir and the family head after Abraham. It was a principle of blood atonement. See JD 4:120.

---

49 See *Genesis* 21:14. cf. *WJS* 245 (this act is what qualified Abraham for his second anointings).

Talent is Adamic for woman.[50]

President John Taylor spoke of the time when the Constitution of the United States would hang as by a thread;[51] the fullness of the Priesthood would also hang as by a thread.[52]

At the 1886 meeting, John Taylor said: Kings and Queens and the rulers of the earth will pay tribute to some of you and your associates. Those who take part in casting you out and are vicious, their names shall be blotted out from the Book of Life.

Satan cannot imitate the voice of God's messengers and deceive the Priesthood.

Russia has so much of the blood of Israel, millions will likely receive the Gospel when the time comes,[53] after which there will probably be a financial fight between Russia and England, the former attacking India and winning.

In the early fifties, Brigham Young said substantially as follows:
"After me will come a man to lead this people who will die a martyr. He will give his life for the same principle that Joseph Smith did; and after his time, men will be raised up who will

---

[50] Joseph Smith taught that the parable of the talents referred to plural marriage. See *WJS*, 269; *Journal of Wilford Woodruff* (10/14/1882); *JD* 16:166; 22:616; *D&C* 132:44 (last phrase).
[51] This famous prophecy is oft believed to come from an unpublished address entitled, "A Few Items from a Discourse Delivered by Joseph Smith, July 19, 1840" that has also been referred to as the White Horse Prophecy. See also *JD* 2:182; 12:204; 21:8. James Burgess was present when this prophecy was given and testified that this statement was true. See *WJS*, 279 (6 May 1843 Note).
[52] Fundamentalists often consider this prophecy to have been fulfilled in Lorin C. Woolley because he was the only member of the council of friends living on December 13, 1928. See *Minutes* 2a. He did not reorganize the council until 1932 and upon completing the council, fell ill and was unable to attend their meetings until his death.
[53] cf. *Minutes* 4a, 8a.

offer their lives for the same principle and they will become martyrs, though they may live to see the Second Coming of Christ."

In Brigham City, at a conference in 1882, probably in early May, George Q. Cannon stated in substance:
When the Constitution of the United States will hang as by a thread, it will not be the politicians or statesmen or political parties that will save it, but it will be saved by the Priesthood of God. This statement was made in the name of the Lord and was endorsed by President John Taylor.

Speaking further, President Cannon cautioned the Saints against building reservoirs in the canyons and placing their homes below them as the storms and earth eruptions would come, breaking the dams, causing flood and great damage to life and property.

Succession in the Presidency:
Joseph Smith designated Hyrum Smith and Brigham Young to succeed him, in the order named.[54]

11 A

Brigham Young designated John Taylor at Manti.
John Taylor designated Wilford Woodruff at Brigham City.
Wilford Woodruff lost power (in consequence of the Manifesto) to designate his successor and Lorenzo Snow was designated by the Lord through Joseph F. Smith, who recommended the name to the Quorum.
Lorenzo Snow designated Joseph F. Smith at Bountiful, stating it had always been his impression that Joseph F. Smith would succeed him. Previous to this, when President Snow was nearly drowned at Hawaii, he claimed to have seen in

54 cf. *Minutes* 8a.

vision that Joseph F. Smith would be President of the Church.
Heber J. Grant stated that President Smith, a few days before his death said, "Because you are President of the Twelve, I expect you to be President of the Church," but President Smith took the Keys to Presidency back with him.

"Friends" have jurisdiction over life and death.

When a man repudiates his Priesthood seven times, it is taken from him by God Himself.

As a continuation of the revelation (D&C 132), the Lord revealed:
"A man dishonoring his Priesthood and his marriage covenants forfeits his wives and children; the wives, being released by the same authority that sealed them, are free to marry other worthy men, their children automatically going to their new husbands without an adoption ceremony. Children follow their mother and her sealing to a husband takes the children with her. Should she remain unmarried after her separation from her unworthy husband, and her father is worthy and living the Gospel, she and her children become his.
Christ's statement (Matt. 5:31-32)[55] indicating fornication and adultery [are] the only grounds for divorce has been modified to mean that a man may become unworthy of his wife and yet not be an adulterer, yet she is justified in leaving him and marrying another, under proper authority.
It is also a part of the revelation that while a man might take ten virgins under a vow of marriage as concubines, yet he is under obligation to have them sealed to him at the first opportunity. Hagar was thus sealed to Abraham after his son was born and she had left Abraham's tent.[56] Melchizedek came to Abraham and instructed him to send for Hagar and

---

[55] In the passage referred to, the Savior paraphrases Moses' alterations to the laws of marriage found in *Deuteronomy* 24:1.
[56] See *Genesis* 21:14.

have her sealed to him. Abraham inquired if such was necessary for his exaltation along with that of the woman. The answer being, "Yes," Abraham complied and Hagar became his real wife the same as Sarah.

One of the original Seven in this dispensation was a Jew, Paul Saul. The Seven was organized before the organization of the Church,[57] and Paul Saul, though a member of the Seven, never joined the Church.

At the time of the meeting of September 27, 1886, during the meeting singing was heard, first by only four or five of the thirteen present, the last song being heard by all present. A quartet sang, "The Birth of Christ," and a double quartet sang, "Birth of Joseph Smith" and the "Seer." Two or three other songs were sung. The singing was beautiful. After the singing ceased, President Taylor remarked, "That is the first time I have heard a heavenly choir."

John Taylor said, "Twinkling of an eye" did not mean the space of time it would take an eye to "twinkle or bat," but two or three days. Christ was changed in the "twinkling of an eye."

12 A ☙

On the 100th anniversary of the Prophet's martyrdom, a sacred council will be held in the Temple in Jackson County, consisting of members of the Sanhedrin, the Grand Council, Patriarchs, etc. In the summer of 1936, the Temple will be ready for ordinance work and will be commenced before the end of 1934.

Foregoing items taken from the private journal of Brother Joseph W. Musser.

---

57 Alpheus Cutler made this identical claim. See *Silencing Mormon Polygamy*, 302-03.

1934

MEETING MINUTES OF

THE SCHOOL OF THE PROPHETS

JANUARY 18, 1934 – MAY 26, 1941[1]

2 B ☙

Minutes of the meeting held Thursday, January 18, 1934.
Place: home of J. Leslie Broadbent.
Time: 7:30 p.m.
J. Leslie Broadbent presiding and Louis A. Kelsch conducting.
Opening prayer offered by J. Leslie Broadbent.
Sacrament administered by Joseph W. Musser and Charles F. Zitting.
Minutes of the previous meeting read and approved.

Joseph W. Musser presented the case of Brother T93 73 "RIKS" and sister J9"1DBFI".
They are having some grave family troubles.
After careful consideration J. Leslie Broadbent moved that John Y. Barlow see Brother 7 and counsel him to let the matter rest with the Lord for the time being.
Vote unanimous.

Brother Byron Harvey Allred has asked the council by letter to Joseph W. Musser to read and criticize the manuscript copy he is sending, concerning a supplement in booklet form to A Leaf in Review. It was decided to meet as soon as possible after the manuscript arrives.

---

1 Page 1b of the *Minutes* is missing, including the title.

Some time was spent in discussing the physical condition of Lorin C. Woolley.

After the business matters had been disposed of, a prayer circle was formed. The one praying standing in the center of the circle.[2] Each prayed in turn as follows: J. Leslie Broadbent, Joseph W. Musser, John Y. Barlow, Charles F. Zitting, Louis A. Kelsch asking the Lord for a confirmation from heaven of their calling.
For several minutes after the prayers had been offered, a united silence was observed.

It was then decided to pray again, each taking his turn as before but changing the order as follows; the brother as mouth standing in the center of the circle to be repeated after by the others. Several minutes of united silence was observed between each prayer, during which time the thoughts were prayerfully directed on the particular blessing sought after. During this order of prayer, the first silent period lasted ten minutes, the rest lasting five minutes.
Three things especially were asked for with the understanding that the Lord's will be done. First, that the Father grant unto the six a knowledge of the truth. Second, if not prepared as a body for that knowledge, that they be helped to speedily prepare for that blessing and that J. Leslie Broadbent be given the confirmation and through him the rest might obtain great blessings and help. Third, Satan was rebuked and commanded to stand rebuked that he should not stand between or interfere with the brethren receiving a confirmation.

The Spirit of the Lord was felt in abundance and each felt that the right course was being pursued.

---

2 It appears that this was the manner in which these prayer circles were usually performed. See *Minutes* 6b, 7b, 8b, 9b, 11b, and 12b.

J. Leslie Broadbent then moved that the purification fast be continued another week and that the food fast be observed, as before, on the following Thursday. Unanimous vote.

Lorin C. Woolley and LeGrand Woolley were absent by excuse.
John Y. Barlow closed the evening with prayer.

3 B

Minutes of the special meeting held Sunday, January 23, 1934.
Place: home of J. Leslie Broadbent.
J. Leslie Broadbent presiding and conducting.
Time: 10:00 a.m.

This meeting called to consider the manuscript of a new booklet by Byron Harvey Allred entitled, "A Catechism of the Authoritative Declaration of the Written Word on God in Refutation of the Official Statement of the First Presidency of the Mormon Church."[3]

After thoughtful consideration of the subjects treated by Byron Harvey Allred, it was deemed best for him not to publish his work at this time.

LeGrand Woolley then moved that Allred be advised not to publish his new booklet now and in an inoffensive way, be given the reasons for such a decision by the council.
This motion was amended by J. Leslie Broadbent to the effect that LeGrand Woolley outline, Joseph W. Musser write, and J. Leslie Broadbent sign the letter. Vote unanimous.

---

[3] This is a reference to the June 17, 1933 official statement from the First Presidency and the Quorum of Twelve Apostles wherein they dispute the authenticity of the 1886 revelation and the priesthood claims of Lorin C. Woolley. That statement contained many inaccuracies concerning the 1886 revelation. See *Silencing Mormon Polygamy*, 137.

J. Leslie Broadbent suggested that we make a careful study of the Doctrine and Covenants, spending part of each weekly meeting for that purpose.

Joseph W. Musser moved to adopt the suggestion of J. Leslie Broadbent and that J. Leslie Broadbent act as class leader. Unanimous vote.

Lorin C. Woolley absent by excuse.
Joseph W. Musser offered the closing prayer.

4 B

Minutes of the meeting held January 25, 1934.
Place: home of J. Leslie Broadbent.
Time: 7:30 p.m.
J. Leslie Broadbent presiding and John Y. Barlow conducting.
Opening prayer offered by Louis A. Kelsch.
Minutes of previous meetings read and approved.

John Y. Barlow gave a report of his visit with Brother T93 73"RIKS".[4]

After regular business matters had been finished, the rite of washing of feet was attended to in the order of seniority of ordination as follows: J. Leslie Broadbent washing the feet of John Y. Barlow and John Y. Barlow of Joseph W. Musser, etc.
Following the washing of feet, a prayer circle was formed. Each, in turn, in order of ordination, stood in the center of the circle and prayed, being repeated after by the rest. Again the Lord was asked to confirm our calling and to grant us a knowledge of the truth for which we are contending.
After the prayers had been offered, while sitting silently and thinking of what had been done, John Y. Barlow asked J. Leslie Broadbent to get up and speak to us, promising him

[4] cf. *Minutes* 2b.

that the Holy Ghost would direct him. John Y. Barlow also called upon the others, in the following order: LeGrand Woolley, Joseph W. Musser, Charles F. Zitting, Louis A. Kelsch, to express their feelings regarding what was being done. John Y. Barlow then speaking himself. J. Leslie Broadbent asked to speak again and did so with the Spirit of the Lord, forgiving our sins and blessing us.

A unanimous vote was made upon motion by Joseph W. Musser to continue the [purification] fast[5] another week.

Lorin C. Woolley was absent by excuse.
Closing prayer offered by Joseph W. Musser.

5 B

Minutes of meeting held February 1, 1934.
Place: home of J. Leslie Broadbent.
Time: 7:30.
J. Leslie Broadbent presiding and Joseph W. Musser conducting.
John Y. Barlow offered the opening prayer.
Louis A. Kelsch and J. Leslie Broadbent administered the Sacrament.
Minutes of previous meeting read and approved.
Lorin C. Woolley and LeGrand Woolley were absent by excuse.

J. Leslie Broadbent read a letter from Byron Harvey Allred of 9E"9J' BR8A3, regarding his manuscript in which Brother Byron Harvey Allred appears to be disappointed with the advice and decision of the Council. The manuscript was not sanctioned because it was tinged with bitterness, lacked charity and indulged in personalities bordering on a betrayal of confidence. Brother Allred says in his letter that he

---

5 cf. *Minutes* 5b

intended to soften such parts of his work as seemed unkind or uncharitable. He says further, that his publishers (JA9 Q8MJ3F, GIBFJ915, DJR. of Q8DR79D," Idaho) demand a fulfillment of his contract and the only way he sees open to meet their demand is to publish his supplement as proposed. His plans were to give this Catechism free with each purchase of A Leaf in Review, thereby creating interest in and increasing the sale of his book, thus discharging his obligations. In closing, he says that unless we can give him more definite and justifiable reason for not publishing his revamped writing, he sees no other means of accomplishing this end.

After reconsidering and discussing the matter, at Brother Allred's request, the Council still felt that he would not be able to accomplish his desires by his present plans.

J. Leslie Broadbent moved that a letter be written Brother Allred to that effect. Also, that our objection to his previous letter is to stand and if he goes ahead, it will be on his own responsibility. Vote unanimous.

J. Leslie Broadbent and Joseph W. Musser are to write the letter.

The time was then turned over to J. Leslie Broadbent for class study. One hour and five minutes was spent reading and discussing the first lecture on faith.

J. Leslie Broadbent advanced the beautiful thought of the relationship of men of the Order of Melchizedek to each other and brought forth scriptural evidence that men of this order would be the final judges of each other. (D&C 107:78-83)

Following this study, a prayer circle was formed. Once again, the Lord was sought for a confirmation of calling. The order of prayer again followed the order of seniority of ordination, the brother as mouth standing in the center of the circle, the others repeating after.

The purification fast as a group fast was discontinued for the time being, this matter now resting with the individual. However, the food fast is to continue on each regular meeting day, to be observed as a group.

Charles F. Zitting offered the closing prayer.

6 B

Minutes of the meeting held at the home of J. Leslie Broadbent.
February 8, 1934.
Time: 7:30 p.m.
J. Leslie Broadbent presiding and Charles F. Zitting conducting.
Opening prayer offered by J. Leslie Broadbent.
Sacrament administered by Louis A. Kelsch and John Y. Barlow.
Minutes of previous meeting read and approved.

The time was turned over to class study, there being no business to attend to. One hour was spent studying the second lecture on faith.

We then formed a prayer circle, following the same procedure as of previous weeks, with the same thought and desire in mind, a knowledge of the Lord.

Some time was spent discussing topics of general interest, such as: world disorders, physical condition of Lorin C. Woolley, our responsibilities and duties, etc.

Closing prayer offered by LeGrand Woolley.

7 B

Minutes of the meeting held at the home of J. Leslie Broadbent. February 15, 1934.
J. Leslie Broadbent presiding and LeGrand Woolley conducting.
Opening prayer was offered by Joseph W. Musser.
Sacrament administered by Charles F. Zitting and John Y. Barlow.
Minutes of previous meeting read and approved.

By request of the Council, Joseph W. Musser has written a brief history of the calling, meetings, and development of this Council, containing in addition, some very important items of doctrinal, historical, and prophetical nature, as they have been given over a period of many months by Lorin C. Woolley. This record was read and discussed.[6]
J. Leslie Broadbent moved that the record, as read, be adopted as part of the regular record and to be kept in strict confidence. Vote unanimous.

J. Leslie Broadbent read a very remarkable dream entitled, "An Instructive Dream," which sister Olive Kunz received on the night of January 30, 1934.

A prayer circle was formed, the same order followed and blessings asked for as at previous meetings.

The next meeting is to be held on Friday, February 23, instead of February 22, which is George Washington's Birthday.
Lorin C. Woolley absent by excuse.
John Y. Barlow closed with prayer.

8 B ☙

---

6 The historical record referred to is undoubtedly the summary of School of the Prophet minutes contained earlier in this volume. The material contained therein has been previously published in *Joseph W. Musser's Book of Remembrance.* That volume contains many more teachings of Lorin C. Woolley and is much larger than the summary contained within this volume.

Minutes of the meeting held February 23, 1934.
Place: home of J. Leslie Broadbent.
J. Leslie Broadbent presiding and Louis A. Kelsch conducting.
Time: 7:30 p.m.
Opening prayer by J. Leslie Broadbent.
Sacrament administered by Joseph W. Musser and John Y. Barlow.
Minutes of previous meeting read and approved.

Brother Kunz has asked Joseph W. Musser to give two members of his family Patriarchal blessings. The question was raised as to what Joseph W. Musser's duty was in the matter. The decision was that the Council functions, at present, only in those matters pertaining to life and salvation that cannot wait until the Church is set in order. Nevertheless, let the Spirit be free in dictating the proper course to pursue.

Discussed the case of Brother T93 73"RIKS"[7] and also the practice of administering the Sacrament in public meetings of excommunicated members. It was deemed best not to engage in this practice under present conditions. If a man, as head of his own home, wishes to administer the Sacrament to his family in private, knowing they are worthy, it is his privilege.

The prayer circle was then formed, the same as on previous occasions.
Lorin C. Woolley and LeGrand Woolley were absent by excuse.
Charles F. Zitting offered the closing prayer.

---

[7] cf. *Minutes* 2b and 4b; this is the third reference in four weeks to this family's struggles.

9 B

Minutes of the meeting held at the home of J. Leslie Broadbent.
March 1, 1934.
J. Leslie Broadbent presiding and conducting.
Time: 7:30 p.m.
Joseph W. Musser opened the meeting with prayer.
Sacrament administered by John Y. Barlow and Louis A. Kelsch.
Minutes of previous meeting read and approved.

In the opening prayer, Joseph W. Musser made a very unusual request. He asked Brother John W. Woolley to intercede with the Heavens on our behalf that we might soon receive a confirmation of our calling. Brother John W. Woolley was thus petitioned because of the physical weaknesses and unhappy condition of Lorin C. Woolley.

Joseph W. Musser reports that he explained the position of the Council, relative to giving Patriarchal blessings, to Brother Kunz, who accepted the explanation in good spirit.

Charles F. Zitting entered the motion that the purification fast be commenced again, immediately, and continued for five weeks.
Vote unanimous.

Fifty minutes was devoted to studying the third and fourth Lectures on Faith.

Discussed the meeting at Brother PKIJ B8ED37'S [Bert] on Sunday, February 25, 1934. Several sisters present said they saw a face like that of the Savior's, as portrayed in pictures, overshadow the face of J. Leslie Broadbent as he spoke. Without knowing this, Joseph W. Musser spoke and proclaimed there were present literal descendents of the Lord Jesus Christ.

Another matter discussed was the practice of some of the brethren offering us money as tithing. This money is not to be formally received as tithing but rather as a donation and the Saints must understand it as such.

Still another subject of interest was the practice of receiving money from the Saints in return for sealing blessings. Two or three cases were mentioned of years gone by, among whom was Brother Mathias Cowley.
None of the Council felt justified in such a practice today.

The prayer circle was then formed as in past weeks.

Joseph W. Musser and J. Leslie Broadbent asked to be blessed for their health. Joseph W. Musser for a bronchial irritation and general weakness of a recent illness and J. Leslie Broadbent for a bronchial irritation of several years standing. Joseph W. Musser was anointed by Charles F. Zitting, sealing by J. Leslie Broadbent. J. Leslie Broadbent was anointed by Joseph W. Musser, sealing by Louis A. Kelsch.

Lorin C. Woolley was absent by excuse.
LeGrand Woolley was excused at 8:30 p.m.
Charles F. Zitting offered the closing prayer.

10 B ☙

Minutes of the meeting held March 8, 1934.
Place: home of J. Leslie Broadbent.
J. Leslie Broadbent presiding and John Y. Barlow conducting.
Opening prayer offered by Louis A. Kelsch.
Sacrament administered by J. Leslie Broadbent and Joseph W. Musser.
Minutes of previous meeting read and approved.

J. Leslie Broadbent reported his visit with Lorin C. Woolley. Lorin C. Woolley says the string has been pulled on the Brethren, referring to the Church indebtedness.

John Y. Barlow recounted two recent dreams: The icy river and the two horses of John Taylor's day.

Brother Boss has asked about having his daughter and step-son baptized. The question was raised as to the propriety of the children of excommunicated Saints being baptized and confirmed members of the Church. Joseph W. Musser referred to what Anthon H. Lund had said, in a prayer meeting in the Temple, since 1900, that children of polygamous marriages should be blessed or baptized and confirmed members of the Church privately and that a home record should be kept, to be reported for Church record at the proper time.
Joseph W. Musser moved that Brother Arnold Boss baptize his daughter and step-son, that Brother Morris Kunz confirm them members of the Church and that Charles F. Zitting confirm all he had previously baptized members of the Church.
Vote unanimous.

Joseph W. Musser presented the following information regarding the origin and authorship of the Lectures on Faith:

December 1, 1834.

"Our School for the Elders was now well attended, and with the Lectures on Theology, which were regularly delivered, absorbed for the time being, everything else of a temporal nature."
Joseph Smith, History of the Church 2:175-76.

"These Lectures on Theology here referred to were afterwards prepared by the Prophet and published in the D&C under the Title – Lectures on Faith."
Note by B. H. Roberts, History of the Church 2:176

"During the month of January (1835), I was engaged in the School of the Elders, and in preparing the Lectures on Theology for publication in the Book of Doctrine and Covenants, which the Committee appointed last September [is] now compiling."
Joseph Smith, History of the Church 2:180

"Elder John Smith, taking the lead of the High Council in Kirtland, bore record that the revelations in said book were true, and that the lectures were judiciously arranged and compiled, and were profitable for doctrine."
History of the Church 2:244

"Statement of Joseph Smith, Oliver Cowdery, Sidney Rigdon and Frederick. G. Williams to the Member of the Church of Latter-day Saints.

Dear Brethren:

We deem it to be unnecessary to entertain you with a lengthy preface to the following volume, (D&C) but merely to say that it contains in short the leading items of the religion which we have professed to believe.
The first of the book will be found to contain a series of lectures as delivered before a theological class in this place, (Kirtland, Ohio) and in consequence of their embracing the important doctrine of Salvation, we have arranged them in to the following work.

11 B

The second part contains (the revelations in the D&C), etc.

History of the Church 2:250

Forty-five minutes was then devoted to studying the fifth Lecture on Faith.

The prayer circle was then formed. The brother as mouth (J. Leslie Broadbent), kneeling, facing the Temple, the rest encircling him and repeating after. The same blessings were asked for as on previous occasions.

Lorin C. Woolley and LeGrand Woolley were absent by excuse.
Joseph W. Musser closed the meeting with prayer.

12 B

Minutes of the meeting held Thursday, March 15, 1934.
Place: home of J. Leslie Broadbent.
J. Leslie Broadbent presiding and Joseph W. Musser conducting.
John Y. Barlow opened the meeting with prayer.
Sacrament administered by LeGrand Woolley and Charles F. Zitting.
Minutes of previous meeting read, some changes made, and approved.

Charles F. Zitting reports he has completed his appointment of last meeting.

J. Leslie Broadbent informs us that Brother Arnold Boss' step-son (Arthur Halliday) is desirous of receiving the Priesthood. J. Leslie Broadbent was appointed to look into the matter more fully.

Joseph W. Musser read part of a letter from Eslie Jenson, EBD"LED"9, and KJ. He is still very appreciative of the visit paid him by the brethren on the occasion of the dedication of his home and is hopefully looking forward to another visit in the near future.

Discussed the earthquakes of the past week, reported to be the worst in the recorded history of this section. (Book of Mormon history excepted.)

Studied thirty minutes on the sixth Lecture on Faith.

LeGrand Woolley told of visiting the Ensign State Conference two weeks ago, at which Presidents Heber J. Grant and J. Reuben Clark were present. The authorities are scolding because of the lack of faith and respect for the authorities on the part of the young people.

J. Leslie Broadbent read a letter from Byron Harvey Allred. He is revising his "Catechism" manuscript and if he can obtain financial backing for its publication, he will first send his revised manuscript for criticism of the Council. Joseph W. Musser is to answer this letter and inquire as to what his immediate financial obligation is to his printer.

The prayer circle was then formed. LeGrand Woolley, as mouth, standing in the center, the others standing encircling him, repeating after. A confirmation and actual knowledge is still the foremost blessing sought after.

Lorin C. Woolley was excused on account of illness.
J. Leslie Broadbent closed with prayer.

13 B ☙

Minutes of the meeting held Thursday, March 22, 1934.
Place: J. Leslie Broadbent home.
Time: 7:30 p.m.
J. Leslie Broadbent presiding and Charles F. Zitting conducting.

Opening prayer offered by John Y. Barlow.
Sacrament administered by Joseph W. Musser and Louis A. Kelsch.
Minutes of previous meeting read and approved.

J. Leslie Broadbent read a letter from Byron Harvey Allred stating that he owes $206.25 to his printer and that it is due April 25, 1934. Byron Harvey Allred also sent his manuscript for the Council to pass on.
LeGrand Woolley moved that we read the manuscript individually, as soon as possible and pass on it then.
Vote unanimous.

The prayer circle was then formed the same as in the last meeting. John Y. Barlow as mouth.

Joseph W. Musser read a pamphlet by IBII 8IF3DR (QDNR9 F9BD53F) entitled, "Steadying The Ark." This is a bitter denunciation of Heber J. Grant and his policies; spiritual, financial, and political. The opinion of the Council is that it is written in the spirit of retaliation, recrimination, and bitterness, and in short, the spirit of hell. Men should stick to principle and not personalities.

Charles F. Zitting read parts of two letters written to relatives of members of his family by county relief workers, misrepresenting the condition of his family, saying they were sick and destitute.

Lorin C. Woolley was excused on account of sickness.
Louis A. Kelsch closed with prayer.

14 B ☙

Minutes of the meeting of March 29, 1934.
Place: home of J. Leslie Broadbent.
Time: 7:30 p.m.

J. Leslie Broadbent presiding and LeGrand Woolley conducting.
Opening prayer by Charles F. Zitting.
Sacrament administered by Joseph W. Musser and J. Leslie Broadbent.
Minutes of previous meeting read and approved.

Discussed Byron Harvey Allred's manuscript.
J. Leslie Broadbent moved that we write him, requesting a copy of his diagram, and finding out if he intends to come in for Conference. If so, we should like to go into the matter with him, personally.
Vote unanimous.

J. Leslie Broadbent presented the case of Prentice Fitzgerald.

Joseph W. Musser reported a visit with Lorin C. Woolley.

We then formed a prayer circle with J. Leslie Broadbent as mouth.

Spent one hour studying the seventh Lecture on Faith.

Lorin C. Woolley and John Y. Barlow were absent by excuse, Lorin C. Woolley for illness, and John Y. Barlow on a trip to Southern Utah.
Louis A. Kelsch closed with prayer.

15 B ☙

Minutes of the meeting held April 5, 1934.
Place: home of J. Leslie Broadbent.
Time: 7:30 p.m.
J. Leslie Broadbent presiding and Louis A. Kelsch conducting.
Opening prayer offered by John Y. Barlow.

Sacrament administered by Charles F. Zitting and Joseph W. Musser.
Minutes of previous meeting read and approved.

J. Leslie Broadbent informed us that Prentice Fitzgerald hadn't gotten in touch with him as yet.

J. Leslie Broadbent recommended that Arthur Halliday be given the Melchizedek Priesthood.
John Y. Barlow moved that Arthur Halliday be given the Melchizedek Priesthood and ordained an Elder.
Vote unanimous.

Joseph W. Musser and J. Leslie Broadbent reported their interview with Abraham Teerlink. He manifested rather a bitter spirit at first but before leaving, appeared desirous of wanting to do what was right.

John Y. Barlow told of his visit to Southern Utah.

J. Leslie Broadbent recounted the experience of 181D C9FJ05QA. He was attacked in his own home by a brother and a friend of his wife.

Joseph W. Musser moved to continue the purification fast one week.
Vote unanimous.

J. Leslie Broadbent read extracts of a purported letter, written to Rulon C. Allred and wife by Abraham W. Smoot, in which Abraham W. Smoot discounts the Revelations of 1880 and 1886 and places the stamp of disapproval upon the principle and practice of plural marriage.

J. Leslie Broadbent read a circular, which has been quite generally distributed, entitled, "A Review," and signed A. N. Observer. It is directed against the present L.D.S. Church General Authorities and also quotes from a sermon delivered in Provo Sixth Ward at 6:30 p.m., March 11, 1934, by J. Golden Kimball. The Council is not in harmony with such publications and does not sanction articles written in a spirit of bitterness and accusation.

Charles F. Zitting read a letter which he received from Samuel Eastman, belittling and discrediting the "Woolley people" and certain men writing books.

Studied Section one of the D&C, also section two.

Prayer Circle. J. Leslie Broadbent as mouth uttered an inspired prayer.

This evening has been one of spiritual feasting.

Lorin C. Woolley and LeGrand Woolley were absent by excuse.
Joseph W. Musser closed with prayer.

16 B

Minutes of a special meeting held April 10, 1934.
Place: J. Leslie Broadbent home.
J. Leslie Broadbent presiding and conducting.
Time: 10:00 a.m.
This meeting called to discuss with Byron Harvey Allred, his manuscript.
Opening prayer offered by Louis A. Kelsch.

J. Leslie Broadbent presented the opinion of the Council and in an inspired manner presented a new plan to Byron Harvey Allred. The plan being that Byron Harvey Allred write, in place of his manuscript a new booklet, dealing with several important items which have arisen of late, among which are: Anthony W. Ivin's letter and information regarding the Revelations of 1880 and 1886. Also that he treat, with the

help and sanction of the Council, all other new points of interest pertaining to the fullness of the Gospel, which are deemed wise to be written at this time. The Council assuming the publication cost and circulation of the work. Byron Harvey Allred was in hearty accord with this plan and expressed joy and thankfulness at being considered worthy of such a responsibility.
Byron Harvey Allred was then set apart for this purpose. Joseph W. Musser as mouth.

Discussed the financial obligations concerning his book, 8DBF1.

Lorin C. Woolley was absent by excuse.
John Y. Barlow closed with prayer.

17 B ☙

Minutes of the meeting held Thursday, April 12, 1934.
Place: home of J. Leslie Broadbent.
Time: 7:30 p.m.
J. Leslie Broadbent presiding and conducting.
Sacrament administered by Louis A. Kelsch and John Y. Barlow.
Minutes of previous meeting were read, some additions made, and approved.

Joseph W. Musser presented the following information concerning the First Section of the D&C:

"Section 1 – D&C given during a Special Conference of Elders of Church of Jesus Christ of L.D.S., held at Hiram, Ohio, November 1, 1831." It was given following Section 66, October 25(?), 1831, and prior to Section 67, given near the same time.
Section one given at the time when publication of "Book of Commandments" was being considered.

(HC 1:222)

Attended to the ordinance of washing of feet. The ordinance was performed as follows: J. Leslie Broadbent for John Y. Barlow; John Y. Barlow for Louis A. Kelsch; Louis A. Kelsch for Joseph W. Musser; Joseph W. Musser for Charles F. Zitting; Charles F. Zitting for J. Leslie Broadbent.

Discussed Charles F. Zitting's case. Relief investigators have been saying that Charles F. Zitting and others are going to be imprisoned because of their marriage relations. It is the impression of the Council that some of the faithful brethren may have to go to jail or prison and that there is persecution in the offing.

Charles F. Zitting raised a question regarding giving of information about the garment. Decision was that this information is not to be given out now.

Prayer circle formed, John Y. Barlow as mouth.
Lorin C. Woolley and LeGrand Woolley excused.
Charles F. Zitting closed with prayer.

18 B

Minutes of the meeting held Thursday, April 19, 1934.
Place: home of J. Leslie Broadbent.
Time: 7:30 p.m.
J. Leslie Broadbent presiding and John Y. Barlow conducting.
Opening prayer offered by Joseph W. Musser.
Sacrament administered by LeGrand Woolley and J. Leslie Broadbent.
Minutes of previous meeting read and approved.

As LeGrand Woolley was absent last meeting, J. Leslie Broadbent performed the ordinance of washing of feet for him.

Charles F. Zitting reported that he had baptized and confirmed more of the Boss family. Also that he met Prentice Fitzgerald, who told Charles F. Zitting that he had had a change of heart and didn't want to marry the woman he had been courting. He says she doesn't approve being married by the Priesthood.
J. Leslie Broadbent had asked the Lord that Prentice Fitzgerald would not come to him unless it was right he should do so, and up to now, he hasn't approached J. Leslie Broadbent.

Joseph W. Musser presented his correspondence with Heber J. Grant of November 1928.
Louis A. Kelsch moved that this correspondence be published in the new booklet and also, that John Y. Barlow's suggestion to use the scripture found in D&C 64:38-39 be accepted. Vote unanimous.

John Y. Barlow told of a recent dream he had in which the Savior led him over a black, muddy, treacherous ground to safety, but only by following in the same footsteps of the Savior was he able to escape certain destruction.

Joseph W. Musser told of a recent dream of his wherein the Savior was visiting with some of the brethren, apparently in a meeting.

Joseph W. Musser said that at three recent meetings, as J. Leslie Broadbent was speaking, several have testified that the face or likeness of the Savior overshadowed his countenance.[8]

LeGrand Woolley told of a recent meeting with J. Golden Kimball and commenting on his talk at the last conference Brother Kimball said his speech was made up of parts of speeches which he had, numbering a hundred or more.

---

[8] One of these meetings was likely held on February 25, 1934. See *Minutes* 9b above.

Prayer circle was then formed, Joseph W. Musser as mouth.
Lorin C. Woolley is still ill and therefore excused. He was worse this past week than at any time since this last illness overtook him.
Louis A. Kelsch closed with prayer.

19 B ☙

Minutes of the meeting held April 26, 1934.
Place: home of J. Leslie Broadbent.
Time: 7:30 p.m.
J. Leslie Broadbent presiding and Joseph W. Musser conducting.
Louis A. Kelsch opened with prayer.
Sacrament administered by John Y. Barlow and J. Leslie Broadbent.
Minutes of previous meeting read and approved.

7BD"9E P8DR9" [William] has asked John Y. Barlow or Edmund Barlow to take full responsibility of his worldly goods in case he dies and he feels like that will be soon. Someone to act as an executor, to make funeral arrangements, etc., and to carry out his instructions honestly and sincerely.
John Y. Barlow was selected for the responsibility.

John Y. Barlow said that Julia Barlow's two sons wanted to be given the Priesthood.
J. Leslie Broadbent moved that Edmund Barlow use his own judgment as to which authority to give them. They are not, however, to receive an office above that of Elder.
Vote unanimous.

J. Leslie Broadbent reported on Lorin C. Woolley's physical condition. He is very weak and lies down most of the time.

Lorin C. Woolley said John W. Taylor had been to see him and told him that Francis R. Lyman was pushing the Abraham Teerlink case but did not have enough power to get a conviction.

Studied Sections 3, 4, 5, and 6 of the D&C.

Prayer circle was then formed with Charles F. Zitting as mouth.
Lorin C. Woolley and LeGrand Woolley were excused.
J. Leslie Broadbent closed with prayer.

20 B

Minutes of the meeting held May 3, 1934.
Place: home of J. Leslie Broadbent.
Time: 7:30 p.m.
J. Leslie Broadbent presiding and Charles F. Zitting conducting.
Joseph W. Musser opened with prayer.
Sacrament administered by John Y. Barlow and Louis A. Kelsch.
Minutes of previous meeting read and approved.

John Y. Barlow reported his findings concerning sister Jesse Porver, a friend and one time school pupil of Byron Harvey Allred.

J. Leslie Broadbent read a letter of the Council (prepared by Joseph W. Musser and J. Leslie Broadbent) to Byron Harvey Allred, relative to Joseph F. Smith's statement of April 1911, concerning plural marriage. This and all other such statements are pure subterfuge and should be labeled as such and set to one side.
John Y. Barlow moved that we sanction the letter as written. Vote unanimous.

LeGrand Woolley read the statements of Lorin C. Woolley and Daniel Bateman regarding the events of September 26 & 27, 1886, when the Revelation of 1886, respecting plural marriage, was given President John Taylor.
LeGrand Woolley moved that the statements, as given, be sent to Byron Harvey Allred to be used in the new publication.
Vote unanimous.
These statements are used, at this time, with the sanction of Lorin C. Woolley and Daniel Bateman.

Discussed topics of general importance and interest.

Prayer circle was then formed, Louis A. Kelsch as mouth.
Lorin C. Woolley absent by excuse.
J. Leslie Broadbent offered the closing prayer.

21 B ☙

Minutes of the meeting held Thursday, May 10, 1934.
Place: home of J. Leslie Broadbent.
Time: 7:30 p.m.
J. Leslie Broadbent presiding and LeGrand Woolley conducting.
Opening prayer offered by John Y. Barlow.
Sacrament administered by Charles F. Zitting and Louis A. Kelsch.
Minutes of previous meeting read and approved.

Discussed the physical condition of Lorin C. Woolley.

It is reported that police officers are after Morris Kunz.
John Y. Barlow moved that J. Leslie Broadbent and LeGrand Woolley go to see H. S. Tanner and find out what help or information he could give in case of arrests.
Unanimous vote.

Charles F. Zitting told of Brother A. B. Robinson being killed by a hit-and-run driver, in Oklahoma.

Studied Sections 8 and 9 of the D&C.

Prayer circle was formed, J. Leslie Broadbent as mouth.
Lorin C. Woolley absent by excuse.
Joseph W. Musser closed with prayer.

22 B

Minutes of the meeting held Thursday, May 17, 1934.
Place: home of J. Leslie Broadbent.
Time: 7:30 p.m.
J. Leslie Broadbent presiding and Louis A. Kelsch conducting.
Opening prayer offered by Joseph W. Musser.
Sacrament administered by J. Leslie Broadbent and John Y. Barlow.
Minutes of previous meeting read and approved.

Studied Section 10, D&C.

Prayer circle, J. Leslie Broadbent as mouth.

Lorin C. Woolley excused. His health is very poor and is failing very noticeably.
Charles F. Zitting closed with prayer.

23 B

Minutes of the meeting held Thursday, May 24, 1934.
Place: J. Leslie Broadbent home.
Time: 7:30 p.m.
J. Leslie Broadbent presiding and conducting.
Opening prayer offered by Charles F. Zitting.

Sacrament administered by John Y. Barlow and Louis A. Kelsch.
Minutes of the previous meeting read and approved.

Discussed the condition of Lorin C. Woolley. He seemed a little improved today, spiritually and physically.

Byron Harvey Allred's manuscript for the new booklet has arrived and been read. For several reasons, among which is the personal affairs of Byron Harvey Allred's son, the Council feels it would be better for the Priesthood to take this fight off of his hands and assume full responsibility for its writing and publication.
Vote unanimous.

J. Leslie Broadbent told of a conversation with Roy Wilson who said he had reliable information that Federal investigators are here from Washington, D.C., trying to get evidence to convict polygamists, but, however, exempting the Authorities of the Church.

Discussed this information and other important, pressing matters at some length.

Joseph W. Musser was mouth for the prayer circle.
Lorin C. Woolley and LeGrand Woolley were absent by excuse.
Louis A. Kelsch closed with prayer.

24 B ☙

Minutes of the meeting held Thursday, May 31, 1934.
Place: home of J. Leslie Broadbent.
Time: 7:30 p.m.
J. Leslie Broadbent presiding and John Y. Barlow conducting.
Opening prayer offered by LeGrand Woolley.

Sacrament administered by J. Leslie Broadbent and Louis A. Kelsch.
Minutes of previous meeting read and approved.

Talked about Lorin C. Woolley's condition. He seemed even more improved today than last week.

J. Leslie Broadbent told of Roy Wilson's desire to interest the polygamists in moving, in a body, to Old Mexico.
The sentiment of the brethren is to stay here and see the fight out.

Joseph W. Musser has the new book completed with the exception of a chapter on Priesthood.

J. Leslie Broadbent told of the case of 3P18BFQA and his experience in court.
The case against him was dismissed.

Studied Sections 11 and 12, D&C.

Prayer circle, Louis A. Kelsch as mouth.

Discussed ways and means of financing the new publication.

Lorin C. Woolley and Joseph W. Musser absent by excuse.

J. Leslie Broadbent closed with prayer, asking for an overflowing scourge to help bring the world to repentance.

25 B ☙

Minutes of the meeting held Thursday, June 7, 1934.
Place: J. Leslie Broadbent home.
Time: 7:30 p.m.
J. Leslie Broadbent presiding and Joseph W. Musser conducting.

J. Leslie Broadbent opened with prayer.
Sacrament administered by John Y. Barlow and Charles F. Zitting.
Minutes of previous meeting read and approved.

J. Leslie Broadbent read the correspondence, for the latter part of May, between the Council and Byron Harvey Allred, informing him that the Council deemed it best to assume the responsibility of the new publication.

J. Leslie Broadbent then read two letters from 158D"19R [Allred] to Roy Wilson telling of the complications arising, in his family, over the plural marriage question.
LeGrand Woolley moved to send Byron Harvey Allred the last letter as written.
Vote unanimous.

J. Leslie Broadbent recommended that Royal Madsen be given the Priesthood and he and his wife sealed by the Priesthood.
This recommendation unanimously approved.

Joseph W. Musser read a chapter, which he has prepared for the new book, entitled, "Persecution Within."

This was discussed at considerable length and the mind of the Council obtained thereon.

LeGrand Woolley was mouth for the prayer circle.
Lorin C. Woolley was absent by excuse. His condition today appeared about the same as three weeks ago.
Louis A. Kelsch offered the closing prayer.

26 B

Minutes of the meeting held Thursday, June 14, 1934.
Place: J. Leslie Broadbent home.

Time: 7:30 p.m.
J. Leslie Broadbent presiding and Charles F. Zitting conducting.
J. Leslie Broadbent opened with prayer.
Sacrament administered by John Y. Barlow and Louis A. Kelsch.
Minutes of previous meeting read, some amendments made and approved.

Charles F. Zitting reported he had completed his appointment regarding Royal Madsen, also the dedication of Arthur Halliday home.

J. Leslie Broadbent told of a conference with CFD9T"9J," who says there are thirty-five polygamous cases being investigated by the County Attorney's Office, that two assistant attorneys are taking the initiative, the real pressure, however, coming from the heads of the L.D.S. Church, Brother Anthony W. Ivins working with the civil authorities.[9] Chief Deputy Black said he wasn't personally interested in the prosecution.

John Y. Barlow recounted an experience of Daniel Bateman on the Temple Block. He was defending the truth when an authority told him he couldn't talk like that on the grounds. Daniel Bateman became indignant at this and called them dirty cowards. Several followed him out to the sidewalk to hear more of the truth.

J. Leslie Broadbent presented a plan for a canyon trip. Those to go are, J. Leslie Broadbent, John Y. Barlow, and Joseph W. Musser, the purpose being to get away from worldly influences and to try and get the will of the Lord direct.
Joseph W. Musser moved to approve this plan of the President.
Vote unanimous.

---

9 See *Minutes* 68b-69b below for further details surrounding this accusation.

Joseph W. Musser presented chapters one to five of his new book.
The Council approved of them as given.
It was decided that J. Leslie Broadbent sign the new book, with Joseph W. Musser, for in the mouth of two or more witnesses shall all things be established.

LeGrand Woolley came before the meeting and after reading, gave hearty approval of the newly prepared work. He was excused before the meeting, as he is making arrangements to leave next Monday to meet his son in New York. His son is returning from completion of an European Mission.

Lorin C. Woolley was also excused. His condition today was the worst thus far. He is unable to stand because of dizziness.

Louis A. Kelsch was mouth for the prayer circle.
Joseph W. Musser closed with prayer.

27 B

Minutes of the meeting held Thursday, June 21, 1934.
Place: in Lamb's Canyon.
Time: 9:20 a.m.
J. Leslie Broadbent presiding and Louis A. Kelsch conducting.
Sacrament administered by Joseph W. Musser and Charles F. Zitting.
Minutes of previous meeting read and approved.

J. Leslie Broadbent read a letter from Byron Harvey Allred, dated June 16, 1934, expressing his anxiety over his financial embarrassment, incurred through his book. He wants the brethren here to sign a note with him, guaranteeing payment of this obligation.
It was suggested that J. Leslie Broadbent write him to the effect that our signatures are involved to such an extent that it

is doubtful whether they would be of any service to him but that his book will be advertised in Joseph W. Musser's new book and thus help to discharge his obligation.

Joseph W. Musser moved to have a gathering of the brethren here next Sunday at 9:00 a.m.
Vote unanimous.

Each, in the following order, bore testimony to the divinity of the work engaged in: John Y. Barlow, Joseph W. Musser, Charles F. Zitting, Louis A. Kelsch, J. Leslie Broadbent.

J. Leslie Broadbent was mouth for the prayer circle.

Discussed John Y. Barlow's dream of the cattle starving for hay, of the call for veterans, and of guiding the cattle to the leaders, who fed them in abundance.

Lorin C. Woolley and LeGrand Woolley were absent by excuse. Lorin C. Woolley appears to become a little more feeble each week and yesterday was in a scolding mood, scolding his family for their lack of respect for him.

The meeting was a Spiritual feast, being held on a bright, sunny hillside, the place having been previously dedicated to the Lord.

Joseph W. Musser closed with prayer.
Time: 12:25 p.m.

28 B

Minutes of a special meeting held Sunday, June 14, 1934.
Place: J. Leslie Broadbent home.
Time: 9:20 p.m.
J. Leslie Broadbent presiding and conducting.
John Y. Barlow opened with prayer.

The meeting tonight was called that we might offer a special prayer for several women folks, who are called before the Federal Authorities, to be questioned regarding their naturalization.

Louis A. Kelsch was mouth in offering the special prayer.

This meeting was called immediately after a 4 ½ hour meeting held at Arnold Boss' home, where the brethren, about 27 in number, were made acquainted with Joseph W. Musser's new book and their financial, as well as moral support, solicited.

Joseph W. Musser closed with prayer.

29 B

Minutes of the meeting held Thursday, June 28, 1934.
Place: J. Leslie Broadbent home.
Time: 8:30 p.m.
J. Leslie Broadbent presiding and conducting.
Louis A. Kelsch opened with prayer.
Sacrament administered by Charles F. Zitting and John Y. Barlow.
Minutes of previous meeting read and approved.

J. Leslie Broadbent reported that an attorney is acting as counsel for the women folk and is appearing before the Federal Authorities with them. The case has not been settled as yet.

J. Leslie Broadbent counseled us to be very careful in speaking to the people and to use the utmost wisdom, saying only those things which pertain to the spirit of the occasion.

Studied Section 13 of the D&C.

Joseph W. Musser was mouth for the prayer circle.

Lorin C. Woolley and LeGrand Woolley were excused.

Lorin C. Woolley grows more feeble each week and unless the Lord works a miracle in his behalf, his remaining days appear to be very few.

J. Leslie Broadbent closed with prayer.

30 B ☙

Minutes of the meeting held Thursday, July 5, 1934.
Place: J. Leslie Broadbent home.
Time: 7:05 p.m.
J. Leslie Broadbent presiding and John Y. Barlow conducting.
Opening prayer offered by Louis A. Kelsch.
Sacrament administered by J. Leslie Broadbent and Joseph W. Musser.
Minutes of previous meeting read and approved.

J. Leslie Broadbent presented the plan to publish about 2,500 copies, in pamphlet form, of the Priesthood chapter and Lorin C. Woolley statement, in addition to the new book. Joseph W. Musser moved that we adopt the suggestion of the President and try to send out about 2,500 copies.
Vote unanimous.

Discussed means of obtaining a 1934 Church Directory. It was learned today that they have been restricted to President of Stakes, Bishops, their counselors, etc.

Lorin C. Woolley condition was discussed. He became unconscious last Sunday about 10:00 a.m. and has been in a state of coma ever since.

Studied Sections 14, 15, 16, & 17 of the D&C.

J. Leslie Broadbent was mouth for the prayer circle.

The Lord is still being petitioned very earnestly to prepare us for a confirmation of our calling, that we may have an actual knowledge of the truth.

Charles F. Zitting offered the closing prayer.

31 B

Minutes of the meeting held Thursday, July 12, 1934.
Place: J. Leslie Broadbent home.
Time: 7:30 p.m.
J. Leslie Broadbent presiding and Joseph W. Musser conducting.
Charles F. Zitting offered the opening prayer.
Sacrament administered by John Y. Barlow and Louis A. Kelsch.
Minutes of the previous meeting read and approved.

Lorin C. Woolley has regained consciousness and is very weak. He seems to be in a dazed condition, recognizing a person only after being told who it is. It is very depressing to go and see him in such a condition.

The advisability of Charles F. Zitting doing a little missionary work in Brigham City was considered but it was thought best to let the new book do that work at present.

Studied Section 19 of the D&C.

J. Leslie Broadbent was mouth for the prayer circle, offering a very comprehensive and timely prayer.
Joseph W. Musser offered the closing prayer.

32 B ☙

Minutes of the meeting held Thursday, July 19, 1934.
Place: J. Leslie Broadbent home.
Time: 7:30 p.m.
J. Leslie Broadbent presiding and LeGrand Woolley conducting. (Charles F. Zitting being up North and LeGrand Woolley having returned from the East.)
John Y. Barlow opened with prayer.
Sacrament administered by Louis A. Kelsch and Joseph W. Musser.

Lorin C. Woolley's condition remains about the same, very weak and just semi-conscious.

One hundred copies of the new book have been finished and delivered to us. Copies were given to those present. The book is entitled, "Supplement to the New and Everlasting Covenant of Marriage."

Discussed "An Open Letter," by A. Hussburg and Jesse Stone, revealing the identity of the rumored seven.

J. Leslie Broadbent suggested that the purification fast be commenced again immediately and continued indefinitely. Vote unanimous.

Joseph W. Musser was mouth for the prayer circle.
Charles F. Zitting was absent by excuse.
J. Leslie Broadbent closed with prayer.

33 B ☙

Minutes of the meeting held Thursday, July 26, 1934.

Place: J. Leslie Broadbent home.
Time: 7:30 p.m.
J. Leslie Broadbent presiding and Charles F. Zitting conducting.
LeGrand Woolley offered the opening prayer.
Sacrament administered by John Y. Barlow and J. Leslie Broadbent.
Minutes of previous meeting read, some corrections made, and approved.

J. Leslie Broadbent reported that seven hundred books have been delivered to date, three hundred being addressed and ready for mailing. The "Priesthood Items" pamphlet is nearly completed and the literature should be in the mail the fore part of next week.
Joseph W. Musser moved that the manner of mailing be left with the President.
Vote unanimous.

Lorin C. Woolley condition today was about the same as last week.

Charles F. Zitting presented a letter from Elden Kingston, which follows a recent visit. Elden Kingston is seeking advice from the council through Charles F. Zitting after disregarding J. Leslie Broadbent's counsel several months ago.
Charles F. Zitting is to answer him and seek a private interview with him when he returns to Salt Lake City.

J. Leslie Broadbent read a good spirited letter from Clyde Gustafson seeking to reconcile the several factions in Idaho with the brethren here.

Joseph W. Musser was mouth for the prayer circle.
Louis A. Kelsch closed with prayer.

34 B ☙

Minutes of the meeting held Thursday, August 2, 1934.
Place: J. Leslie Broadbent home.
Time: 7:30 p.m.
J. Leslie Broadbent presiding and Louis A. Kelsch conducting.
John Y. Barlow opened with prayer.
Sacrament administered by Charles F. Zitting and Joseph W. Musser.
Minutes of the previous meeting read and approved.

Roy Athey desired to have the Priesthood conferred upon him.
John Y. Barlow moved that the matter be left with J. Leslie Broadbent.
Vote unanimous.

J. Leslie Broadbent reports the printing has been completed, the books and pamphlets delivered to us, and a copy of either the book or pamphlet sent to approximately 1800 authorities in the Church.

Joseph W. Musser told of Bert Biglow's concern over his Priesthood, sealings, endowments, etc. He feels that if the Priesthood wasn't properly conferred upon him, that the other acts of the Priesthood haven't been binding.
Joseph W. Musser moved that John Y. Barlow be given charge of the matter.
Vote unanimous.

Joseph W. Musser saw Roy Wilson today and he appeared in a friendly, pleasant spirit.

Charles F. Zitting told of his chance meeting in the Temple Square Hotel, with an Armenian doctor from Detroit. The doctor was very favorable to the principle of plural marriage.

The purification fast was discussed at considerable length.

Joseph W. Musser moved the fast be continued until the President felt inspired that it had continued long enough. Vote unanimous.

J. Leslie Broadbent was mouth for the prayer circle.

Lorin C. Woolley showed considerable improvement today, the most encouraging since his last weakness began about five weeks ago.

LeGrand Woolley was absent by excuse.
Charles F. Zitting closed with prayer.

35 B

Minutes of the meeting held Thursday, August 9, 1934.
Place: J. Leslie Broadbent home.
Time: 7:30 p.m.
J. Leslie Broadbent presiding and conducting.
John Y. Barlow offered the opening prayer.
Sacrament administered by Charles F. Zitting and Louis A. Kelsch.
Minutes of previous meeting read and approved.

Charles F. Zitting read a letter from the Home Owner's Loan Office in Salt Lake, refusing him a loan, showing how they discriminate against plural families.

Charles F. Zitting also read another letter from his younger sister in Los Angeles. She asks about being sealed to a young man whom she was about to marry but who died of pneumonia.
Charles F. Zitting is to encourage her to not make haste in this matter but to think it over very seriously because this life is the place to live the laws of Salvation.

Joseph W. Musser read a letter to J. Leslie Broadbent from Byron Harvey Allred. He appears considerably put out over certain parts of the new book, "Supplement," and also over the manner in which his manuscript was handled. Brother Byron Harvey Allred is laboring under a gross misunderstanding.
J. Leslie Broadbent then read an answering letter, written in a most kind and understanding manner.
LeGrand Woolley moved that the answer be sent as read. Vote unanimous.

J. Leslie Broadbent read a letter to John Cummard, First Counselor in the Maricopa Stake, Mesa, Arizona, in answer to this thoughtless letter to us, reading the "sky-blue" book. A copy of the correspondence was also sent to the President and Second Counselor of said stake.

Comments both for and against the new work are coming in. The fence is getting higher and higher and slowly but surely the lines are forming, for or against.

J. Leslie Broadbent read the law of retribution as contained in D&C Section 98 and said that law had been fully complied with on his part as had it also been fulfilled by the Church Leaders. The fourth offense committed by them was made upon a member of his family, the notice of excommunication being placed between that of a murderer and an apostate. Joseph W. Musser moved that a testimony against the leaders be brought before the Lord, leaving the matter in His hands. Vote unanimous.

This is the first case, in our experience, of which we have knowledge, wherein all the conditions pertaining to the law of retribution, both for and against, have been fulfilled.

J. Leslie Broadbent asked that we continue the purification fast another week, that we seek the Lord diligently at least

twice daily, until next meeting, and try to obtain the mind and will of the Lord in the matter.
Joseph W. Musser moved we follow this suggestion.
Vote unanimous.

J. Leslie Broadbent reports that C. and Elden Kingston and Clyde Gustafson are in full accord with us and that they desire to line up with the truth. Charles F. Zitting is to attend to some matters for them.

Joseph W. Musser, as mouth for the prayer circle, laid the testimonies against Heber J. Grant and Anthony W. Ivins and all others who have taken part in fighting the Celestial laws, before the Lord.

J. Leslie Broadbent read an article, which John Y. Barlow discovered, written by Joseph Fielding Smith and published in volume two of "Scrapbook of Mormon Literature," attempting to answer the question "Who ordained B. Young President of the Church."[10] Another read article to sustain the idea of a special group of Priesthood, chosen directly by the Lord, and through whom came the succession to the Keys of the Priesthood.

---

10 It appears that this article is located in Rich, Ben E., *A Scrapbook of Mormon Literature,* (Henry C. Etten & Co.: N.D.) 2:460-463 and is entitled "A Word About Succession." On page 462 of that article, the undisclosed author refers to the winter of 1843-44 as the time when Brigham Young received all of the keys necessary to "preside over the high priesthood." Again, this reference is vague but this term was used to refer to the Quorum of Anointed in several journals of the era. Because the context of the minutes entry is somewhat unclear, it is possible that this article is not the same article referred to in the language above. However, the nexus is unmistakable and supports the conclusion that this is the article referred to in the minutes and the conclusion that these keys referred to have some connection to the Quorum of Anointed.
As a tangentially interesting matter, there is no mention in the article of any priesthood "chosen directly by the Lord, and through whom came the succession to the Keys of the Priesthood" in those terms. However, there is an engaging discussion over the Last Charge (it cites *T&S* 5:561, 664, 698 and *MS* 10:115), the succession crisis of 1844, and the "keys of the kingdom" in connection with *D&C* 107:23-24. A cursory glance over *D&C* 107:23-24 and the surrounding verses reveals that no "keys of the kingdom" are referred to in those verses and that only the "power of three presidents" of the Church is referred to.

Lorin C. Woolley condition remains about the same as of last week.

LeGrand Woolley offered the closing prayer.

36 B

Minutes of the meeting held Thursday, August 16, 1934.
Place: J. Leslie Broadbent home.
Time: 7:30 p.m.
J. Leslie Broadbent presiding and John Y. Barlow conducting.
Opening prayer was offered by Joseph W. Musser.
Sacrament administered by J. Leslie Broadbent and John Y. Barlow.
Reading of the minutes of previous meeting deferred until next week.

John Y. Barlow told of a testimony which came to him during the week. He was impressed to read the scriptures on the question of retribution, and that we should leave it in the hands of the Lord, the responsibility being on Him and not us. Felt we had done our part and now it is up to the Lord.

Charles F. Zitting came in at this juncture.

Preceded with lesson, studying balance of Section 19, D&C.

LeGrand Woolley came in at this time.

Lorin C. Woolley appears considerably weaker at this time.

Louis A. Kelsch was excused.
Charles F. Zitting closed with prayer.

37 B

Minutes of the meeting held Thursday, August 23, 1934.
Place: J. Leslie Broadbent home.
Time: 7:30 p.m.
J. Leslie Broadbent presiding and Joseph W. Musser conducting.
Minutes of the previous meeting read and approved.

Joseph W. Musser gave a report of a recent trip to Idaho. He visited Byron Harvey Allred and an amiable understanding was reached.

Sister Ballard was miraculously healed of a high fever after being administered to.

J. Leslie Broadbent read from Section 68, D&C showing who may officiate in the office of Bishop.

Brother Eslie Jenson wants his Priesthood calling made sure.
J. Leslie Broadbent recommended it be done.
LeGrand Woolley moved to follow the recommendation.
Vote unanimous.

Continued study of Section 19, D&C for the lesson.

J. Leslie Broadbent was mouth for the prayer circle.

Charles F. Zitting absent by excuse.

Lorin C. Woolley's condition remains the same as last week.

Louis A. Kelsch closed with prayer.

38 B

Minutes of the meeting held Thursday, August 30, 1934.
Place: J. Leslie Broadbent home.
Time: 7:30 p.m.

J. Leslie Broadbent presiding and Charles F. Zitting conducting
J. Leslie Broadbent opened with prayer.
Sacrament administered by Joseph W. Musser and Louis A. Kelsch.
Minutes of the previous meeting read and approved.
LeGrand Woolley absent by excuse.

Charles F. Zitting told of a chance meeting with C. Nielson and C. Kimball. They manifested disbelief in a Sanhedrin, claiming J. Leslie Broadbent originated it; they also took exception to the Priesthood chapter of the new book. Charles F. Zitting bore his testimony to them and they stopped their complaining. Chase leaving and walking up the street very hurriedly.

LeRoy Wilson said to Charles F. Zitting, during a visit, "look at your man Lorin Woolley, are you proud of him" we thought he was going to take Heber J. Grant's place. Later, Charles F. Zitting had a vision, while watering his crops, in which he saw Roy pointing to the Savior on the cross saying "look at him, he was to be King of this world, are you proud of him now?"

Discussed the book "Holy Murder," purporting to be some inside facts about Porter Rockwell and the Danites.

Louis A. Kelsch excused at this point.

Joseph W. Musser asked for counsel on the propriety of his engaging in selling stock for an oil company as a means of providing for his families. Brethren felt in the absence of direction from the Lord, we cannot instruct against such activities but we should be careful not to injure our Priesthood callings by entering into questionable promotions or other business engagements. These suggestions were given general application so far as members of the Council are concerned.

President J. Leslie Broadbent gave counsel with reference to our actions along all lines, not to destroy our influence among the Saints, and particularly with reference to our attention to women. We must guard carefully the dignity of our calling. We are as a light on a hill, and all are watching us, many with the hope of finding fault.

Regular lesson deferred.

John Y. Barlow was mouth for the prayer circle.

Lorin C. Woolley is still in the same condition.

Joseph W. Musser dismissed.

39 B ☙

Minutes of the meeting held Thursday, September 6, 1934.
Place: J. Leslie Broadbent home.
Time: 7:30 p.m.
J. Leslie Broadbent presiding and Louis A. Kelsch conducting.
Charles F. Zitting offered the opening prayer.
Sacrament administered by Joseph W. Musser and J. Leslie Broadbent.
Minutes of the previous meeting read and approved.

Q1BFT5J3F [Kingston], through Charles F. Zitting, asks direction regarding working among the Lamanites.

J. Leslie Broadbent said we cannot give direction such as that at this time.

John Y. Barlow said we are waiting for light and have gone about as far as we can go.

J. Leslie Broadbent told of Byron Harvey Allred's long letter setting forth his objections and arguments against some items in the new book. John Y. Barlow said new wine cannot be put in old bottles.

LeGrand Woolley came in at this time.

Studied Section 20, D&C.

J. Leslie Broadbent moved, that if possible and consistent, no one is to be given the Priesthood by a member of this Council without first consulting with the Council.
Vote unanimous.

John Y. Barlow was mouth for the prayer circle.
Lorin C. Woolley's condition remains about the same as last week.
J. Leslie Broadbent closed with prayer.

40 B

Minutes of the meeting held Thursday, September 13, 1934.
Place: J. Leslie Broadbent home.
Time: 7:30 p.m.
J. Leslie Broadbent presiding and conducting.
John Y. Barlow opened with prayer.
Sacrament administered by Joseph W. Musser and Louis A. Kelsch.
Minutes of the previous meeting read and approved.

LeGrand Woolley absent by excuse.

Charles F. Zitting informed us that J. Hart told him Charles Hart was in a hopeless physical condition, that death would be a blessing.

Charles F. Zitting also told of Sister Robinson's desire to have her apartment dedicated.
Joseph W. Musser moved that Charles F. Zitting dedicate her apartment.
Unanimous vote.
He is to invite Morris Kunz and wife to go with him.

Louis A. Kelsch read a pamphlet by G. T. Harrison entitled "Mormon Tithing." The Council feels that it is a timely contribution.

J. Leslie Broadbent read Section 119, D&C on Tithing.

J. Leslie Broadbent related an odd dream of his in which he was setting a mercantile institution in a business like order also finding many new tools under a straw pile in the rear of the store, the outstanding tool being pruning snips that hadn't been used, and being asked to call Melvin J. Ballard on the phone to see them.

Charles F. Zitting was mouth for the prayer circle.

Discussed Lorin C. Woolley's condition and the advisability of meeting with the brethren and having special prayers in his behalf.
The Council seems to feel that the Lord's will be done is the safety course to pursue in this present situation.

Discussed Dan Bateman and his spiritual condition.
J. Leslie Broadbent said his case was an illustration to prove that a man cannot become a Son of God without entering into the principle of plural marriage.

Joseph W. Musser closed with prayer.

41 B

Minutes of the meeting held Thursday, September 20, 1934.
Place: J. Leslie Broadbent home.
Time: 7:30 p.m.
J. Leslie Broadbent presiding and John Y. Barlow conducting.
Joseph W. Musser offered the opening prayer.
Sacrament administered by Charles F. Zitting and Louis A. Kelsch.
Minutes of the previous meeting read and approved.

Louis A. Kelsch informed us that the new book is all paid for now excepting $10.20.

J. Leslie Broadbent presented the case of Burt Frandson who desires the Priesthood.
Joseph W. Musser moved that J. Leslie Broadbent take care of that matter for him.
Vote unanimous.

Lorin C. Woolley passed peacefully away yesterday (Wednesday September 19, 1934) at 11:30 a.m. He had weakened quite rapidly since the first of the week.

J. Leslie Broadbent counseled us to be very careful not to make any claims now that Lorin C. Woolley is gone. If we are pressed for an answer just tell them that what we have to say is in the new book.

It was reported by J. Leslie Broadbent and Joseph W. Musser that they had offered the services of the Priesthood to Lorin C. Woolley's family and had advised them of Lorin C. Woolley's aversion to being buried from the Church house.

Joseph W. Musser moved that we commence a purity fast now and continue until further action and that we observe a food fast next Thursday.
Vote unanimous.

J. Leslie Broadbent was mouth for the prayer circle.

LeGrand Woolley was absent by excuse.
John Y. Barlow dismissed.

42 B

Minutes of the meeting held Thursday, September 27, 1934.
Place: J. Leslie Broadbent home.
Time: 7:30 p.m.
J. Leslie Broadbent presiding and Joseph W. Musser conducting.
Sacrament administered by John Y. Barlow and LeGrand Woolley.
Minutes of the previous meeting read and approved.

Discussed the funeral services of Anthony W. Ivins who died last Sunday (September 23, 1934) at 4:30 a.m. The services were probably the most elaborate ever held in the Tabernacle and yet they were devoid of the spirit of the Lord.

Joseph W. Musser recounted his experience before the Twelve, during a five hour meeting in the Temple, about the year 1909. Anthony W. Ivins and Heber J. Grant were trying to get him ousted because he was, as Heber said, in rebellion to them. The question in dispute was plural marriage. Several of the Twelve were befriending Joseph W. Musser, sustaining him in his course.

LeGrand Woolley observed that we are now beginning a new chapter in the record of events. Lorin C. Woolley is gone, having been buried from the Centerville First Ward last Sunday at 2:00 p.m., and according to our understanding, the only mortal man left who actually knew the Lord Jesus Christ and was anointed by Him.

Testimonies were born by the brethren as follows: John Y. Barlow, Charles F. Zitting, Louis A. Kelsch, LeGrand Woolley, Joseph W. Musser, and J. Leslie Broadbent.

John Y. Barlow prophesied that no matter what opposition we encounter, we will not be stopped in our furtherance of the work of the Lord.

J. Leslie Broadbent as mouth for the prayer circle restated our position before the Lord and made further request for a confirmation of our calling.

Charles F. Zitting dismissed.

43 B

Minutes of the meeting held Thursday, October 5, 1934.
Place: J. Leslie Broadbent home.
Time: 7:30 p.m.
J. Leslie Broadbent presiding and Charles F. Zitting conducting.
John Y. Barlow opened with prayer.
Sacrament administered by J. Leslie Broadbent and LeGrand Woolley.
Minutes of the previous meeting read and approved.

Joseph W. Musser absent by excuse.

The matter of gathering in the homes of the brethren to hold meetings was brought up. The attitude of the Council was not to sponsor such meetings regularly, but rather to curtail them somewhat and to proceed very cautiously as we have not, as yet, been sent. To encourage the people to go to their ward chapels when possible to associate and mingle with their neighbors of the ward was deemed a good policy to following during these times of uncertainty.

Discussed the praise of man given Anthony W. Ivins. Four pages of the Monday Tribune (September 24) were devoted to his praise, the publisher of the Tribune (a Catholic) spoke at his funeral service, motion pictures were taken of the affair and as the cortege passed the Catholic Cathedral, the Bishop and Priests in their robes, paid him homage, to the tolling of the Cathedral bells. The pictures are being shown in the Orpheum Theatre this week. Anthony W. Ivins was paid very highly in things that men esteem highly.

Studied Section 20, D&C, verse 68 to end.
LeGrand Woolley was mouth for the prayer circle.
Louis A. Kelsch dismissed with prayer.

44 B ৩

Minutes of the meeting held Thursday, October 12, 1934.
Place: J. Leslie Broadbent home.
Time: 7:30 p.m.
J. Leslie Broadbent presiding and Louis A. Kelsch conducting.
Sacrament administered by J. Leslie Broadbent and John Y. Barlow.
Minutes of the previous meeting read and approved.

Commencing this evening, in administering the Sacrament, the Council knelt with the one saying the blessing on the bread and wine.

Henceforth, the meetings will be commenced promptly at 7:30 p.m. Tardy members will be shown the minutes as such as will also those who are absent without excuse.

Joseph W. Musser moved that the purification fast be discontinued as a Council.
Vote unanimous.

For the lesson, Charles F. Zitting was to find out what he could on the question, should the one performing a baptism go down into the water and come forth up out of the water again with each candidate or not? Nothing definite being shown, the answer was left unsettled.

Louis A. Kelsch was to answer the question, should the bread be blessed before it is broken or after. Left unsettled.

Joseph W. Musser moved that it be the policy of the Council to kneel, as a body, when the Sacrament is being administered to.
Vote unanimous.

J. Leslie Broadbent presented a plan to the Council for their approval, a plan which would be presented to the Lord as one which the Council would be willing to follow in an endeavor to help redeem the people. The plan presented was as follows:
To seek an interview with the authorities of the Church by a letter, over the signatures of all the members of the Council. Should this written request be denied or ignored, the Council will then, in person, as a body, seek an interview with the authorities of the Church at one of their regular Thursday meetings. In case we are denied an interview, the Council is to request judgments at the hands of the Lord, such as are necessary to obtain the interview. In case the request is granted, the Council will then request further opportunity to deliver its message to the General Body of the Priesthood and in turn to the General Conference of the Church.
Any denials of the foregoing requests to incur the judgments of God until such requests are granted so far as it lies within the power of the Council to call forth such judgments. This to be done with the endorsement of Heaven by way of personal and direct knowledge to the one holding the Keys or such of the members of the Council as the Lord sees fit to choose for such knowledge.

Joseph W. Musser moved that the plan be adopted to present to the Lord.
Vote unanimous.
J. Leslie Broadbent as mouth for the prayer circle, presented the plan to the Lord, at which time the Council pledged their lives to carry out the plan should the plan be found acceptable to the Lord. The Council all knelt instead of standing in the circle this evening.

LeGrand Woolley dismissed with prayer.

45 B

Minutes of the meeting held Thursday, October 18, 1934.
Place: J. Leslie Broadbent home.
J. Leslie Broadbent presiding and conducting.
Opening prayer offered by Joseph W. Musser.
Sacrament administered by Charles F. Zitting and Louis A. Kelsch.
Minutes of the previous meeting read, some amendments made, and approved.

John Y. Barlow related his and Edmund Barlow experience, as witnesses, with the stake authorities in the excommunication of Brother William Baldee, showing the unfair, high-handed manner in which he was cast out of the church. President Beesley said it wasn't a question of whether he was right or wrong but rather, was he in harmony with the church leaders.

John Y. Barlow said there was no defense there and the accused was not permitted to discuss or present his views.

For the lesson, studied Sections 21 and 22, D&C.
John Y. Barlow was mouth for the prayer circle.
LeGrand Woolley absent by excuse.
Louis A. Kelsch dismissed with prayer.

46 B ᴄᴣ

Minutes of the meeting held Thursday, October 25, 1934.
Place: J. Leslie Broadbent home.
Time: 7:30 p.m.
John Y. Barlow conducting and J. Leslie Broadbent presiding.
Louis A. Kelsch opened with prayer.
Sacrament administered by Joseph W. Musser and Charles F. Zitting.
Minutes of the previous meeting read and approved.

Louis A. Kelsch raised the question about women going to the Temple to receive endowments before being married. J. Leslie Broadbent observed that no one, other than a legal husband, has the right to take a woman through the veil at the time she receives her new name.

LeGrand Woolley came in at this point.

Of late years, Lorin C. Woolley has held to the idea that only the legal husband has authority to take a wife through the veil. The general opinion of the Council was that under the present conditions, it was best to abide ones time and wait until they can be done properly and in order.

J. Leslie Broadbent asked LeGrand Woolley to read the Patriarchal blessing given by Joseph Smith, Senior upon the head of John W. Woolley.
Copies of the blessing were given to the brethren.

Charles F. Zitting explained the situation between David O. McKay and Charles Owen.

Studied Sections 23 and 24 of the D&C.
J. Leslie Broadbent was mouth for the prayer circle.
LeGrand Woolley dismissed with prayer.

47 B

Minutes of the meeting held Thursday, November 1, 1934.
Place: J. Leslie Broadbent home.
Time: 7:30 p.m.
J. Leslie Broadbent presiding and Joseph W. Musser conducting.
Sacrament administered by John Y. Barlow and J. Leslie Broadbent.
Minutes of the previous meeting read, some additions made, and approved.

Discussed the feasibility of issuing a small monthly publication setting forth items of interest pertinent to present conditions.
No definite action was taken other than to consider the plan for near future action.

Charles F. Zitting asked what lineage to follow in tracing his genealogy after explaining the situation that existed with his grandfather and grandmother.

For the lesson, studied Sections 25 and 26 of the D&C.
Louis A. Kelsch was mouth for the prayer circle.
John Y. Barlow offered the closing prayer.

48 B

Minutes of the meeting held Thursday, November 8, 1934.
Place: J. Leslie Broadbent home.
Time: 7:30 p.m.
J. Leslie Broadbent presiding and Charles F. Zitting conducting.
Sacrament administered by John Y. Barlow and J. Leslie Broadbent.

Louis A. Kelsch came in at this point. Tardiness excused. Minutes of the previous meeting read and approved.

Discussed the lengths to which those opposed to plural marriage will go in order to break the polygamists both spiritually and financially. Charles F. Zitting is about to lose one of his homes because he cannot get a government loan due to such discrimination. John Y. Barlow lost a fine farm for that reason a few years ago.

Some time was spent commenting on current events of special interest.

J. Leslie Broadbent suggested that we read, and did read, the epistle written by Joseph Smith and others while in the Liberty jail. The wisdom of the epistle is a testimony to Joseph's divine mission.

Louis A. Kelsch was mouth for the prayer circle.
LeGrand Woolley was absent by excuse.

J. Leslie Broadbent moved that the purification fast be an individual matter until next Thursday at which time it shall be decided upon as to whether the Council as a whole, wants to commence the fast again for a season.
Unanimous vote.

J. Leslie Broadbent offered the closing prayer.

49 B

Minutes of the meeting held Thursday, November 15, 1934.
Place: J. Leslie Broadbent home.
Time: 7:30 p.m.
J. Leslie Broadbent presiding and LeGrand Woolley conducting.
John Y. Barlow offered the opening prayer.

Sacrament administered by Charles F. Zitting and Louis A. Kelsch.

Louis A. Kelsch moved that the purification fast be observed as a Council until a week next Wednesday on which day we observe a food fast. The meeting to be Wednesday instead of Thursday due to Thanksgiving.
Unanimous vote.

Louis A. Kelsch has received notice to appear before the Stake High Council next Wednesday, November 21, 1934 at 8:00 p.m. at the Granite Stake Tabernacle, to answer a charge of advocating plural marriage. The complaint being made by Russell Wight, a block teaching supervisor in the Wasatch Ward.

J. Leslie Broadbent suggested this plan to follow at the trial:

When asked if guilty or not guilty, Louis A. Kelsch is to ask for a D&C. First, in order to get it in the record and to kill the Manifesto, quote Joseph Smith where he says if anything should have been suggested by us except by commandment or thus saith the Lord, we do not consider it binding.[11] Then, slowly turn to the 132 Section of the D&C, and, after telling the High Council that the D&C advocates plural marriage and as long as that Section is in the D&C, their course is inconsistent, tear the whole Section out, after which have no more to say.
Joseph W. Musser moved that the plan be accepted and followed.
Vote unanimous.

Joseph W. Musser read a letter from Brother Bistline asking questions on Priesthood organization with special regard to the organization of the first Presidency in March 1833.

---

[11] This statement by Joseph Smith is recorded in *HC* 3:295.

Joseph W. Musser also read a letter from Brother Lewis H. Baker from Los Angeles. He has recently published a book called "Highlights of the Book of Mormon."

J. Leslie Broadbent was mouth for the prayer circle.
Charles F. Zitting closed with prayer.

50 B

Minutes of the meeting held Thursday, November 22, 1934.
Place: J. Leslie Broadbent home.
Time: 7:30 p.m.
J. Leslie Broadbent presiding and conducting.
Opening prayer offered by LeGrand Woolley.
Sacrament administered by John Y. Barlow and Charles F. Zitting.

Proceedings of trial of Louis A. Kelsch. November 21, 1934, were read and upon motion of LeGrand Woolley approved and ordered entered in the record.

LeGrand Woolley read from Journal History, dated 1886, a reply of forty-nine inmates in the Utah Penitentiary for the offense of polygamy and unlawful cohabitation, to Governor Caleb West's offer of amnesty if they would comply with the law, in which the brethren all declined the offer of the Governor.

J. Leslie Broadbent read a letter from Byron Harvey Allred indicating a friendly attitude toward our work, and making inquiry with reference to the feasibility of those living the law of Celestial Marriage, colonizing where a united effort for protection and progress may be made and suggesting a location in northwest United States and southwest Canada. Decided we can do nothing until the Lord directs.

J. Leslie Broadbent presented the question of getting out a Second Edition of the Priesthood pamphlet, since the First Edition is about exhausted, also certain additions to clarify parts therein. Also to include the fifth Chapter on Kingdom. Motion of LeGrand decided to get out an additional 2,000 as suggested.
Vote unanimous.

Louis A. Kelsch came in at this point. Excused.

Minutes of the previous meeting read and approved.

Joseph W. Musser as mouth for the prayer circle witnessed before the Lord the proceedings of Louis A. Kelsch trial, also calling attention to the conditions as they stand today.

Louis A. Kelsch closed with prayer.

Account of Louis A. Kelsch's Trial.

Date: November 21, 1934.
Place: Granite Stake Tabernacle. 9th East and Hollywood Avenue
Time: 8:00 p.m.

Louis A. Kelsch was tried before the High Council of the Granite Stake of Zion, Hugh B. Brown, President, on the charge of advocating plural marriage.
Witnesses accompanying Brother Kelsch, Roy Athey, Morris Kunz and Royal Madsen.

After organizing for the trial, the defendant was asked to plead to the charge. Asking for a book of Doctrine and Covenants, Brother Kelsch had the same identified by the President of the Council as the law book of the Church, whereupon he proceeded to demurrer to the sufficiency of the Complaint. Turning to the Woodruff Manifesto, he showed it to be a document unauthorized by the Lord, setting forth the personal views of Wilford Woodruff and his promise to obey the law. Read from a statement of Joseph Smith to the effect that "if anything should be suggested other than the Commandment or thus saith the Lord, we do not [continued next page]

50 B (CONT.) ☙

consider it binding," hence the Manifesto is not binding.[12]

The defendant then turned to Section 132, dealing with the principle of Celestial Marriage, and stated in substance: This section in the D&C advocates plural marriage, and when you handle a person for advocating plural marriage, as long as this section remains in the book, it having been given by "thus saith the Lord," you are forfeiting your priesthood, for the Lord says when we exercise our Priesthood in any degree of unrighteousness, "Amen to the priesthood or the authority of that man." This Section apparently, then, means more to me than it does to you, brethren, and to proceed to handle me for advocating the word of the Lord as contained in this section, this is what you are doing to the word and law of the Lord: The defendant then deliberately tore the revelation from the book, folded it and placed it in his pocket, returning the book to the table where it belonged, and saying, "That is all I have to say."
The Council sat amazed at the audaciousness of the procedure, and after regaining their breaths and asking a number of related questions, the defendant was invited to withdraw to the hallway while the court proceeded to cast a pre-determined vote of "guilty."

---

12 Again, see *HC* 3:295.

The entire proceeding was facial and of a Kangaroo nature, there being no disposition to be guided by the law of the Lord in such hearings.
Thus was President Louis A. Kelsch, a friend and apostle of Jesus Christ – clothed with patriarchal authority, including the sealing powers of heaven – made an ecclesiastical outcast, with the gracious understanding, however, that at any time he felt to repudiate and denounce certain parts of the Gospel of the Lord Jesus Christ, and his revelations pertaining thereto, he might again seek the friendly shelter of the Church Sanctuary, where the brethren would be waiting with open arms to receive him back in full fellowship.

And thus was the fourth glaring offense committed by the officers of the Church of Jesus Christ of Latter-day Saints, against men of the Apostolic order of Joseph Smith:[13] viz: John W. Woolley, Lorin C. Woolley, Joseph Leslie Broadbent, and Louis A. Kelsch, having been handled and cast out from the Church, for sustaining laws of God, this last offense having been committed since the publication of the Supplement to the New and Everlasting Covenant of Marriage, in which authoritative warning had been given.

The vote of excommunication was reported to be unanimous.

51 B

Minutes of the meeting held Thursday, November 28, 1934.
Place: J. Leslie Broadbent home.
Time: 7:30 p.m.
J. Leslie Broadbent presiding and John Y. Barlow conducting.
Opening prayer offered by Louis A. Kelsch.
Sacrament administered by LeGrand Woolley and Joseph W. Musser.

---

13 See *JD* 3:212 for a statement where Brigham Young proclaims himself as an apostle of Joseph Smith.

Minutes of the previous meeting read and approved.

J. Leslie Broadbent says Brother P18BFB9A has asked the permission to ordain his son a deacon.
Joseph W. Musser moves that he go ahead.
Vote unanimous.

J. Leslie Broadbent reported that the contract has been let for two thousand Second Edition Priesthood pamphlets, to cost $84 for printing and about $32.50 for postage.

Charles F. Zitting asked about having a meeting at his Taylorsville home next Sunday. The Council felt it unwise to hold meetings at the present time.

The ordinance of feet washing was then attended to as follows: J. Leslie Broadbent for Louis A. Kelsch, Louis A. Kelsch for LeGrand Woolley, LeGrand Woolley for Joseph W. Musser, Joseph W. Musser for John Y. Barlow, John Y. Barlow for Charles F. Zitting, Charles F. Zitting for J. Leslie Broadbent.

J. Leslie Broadbent as mouth for the prayer circle pled with the Lord for a "confirmation of our calling." The Council knelt in a circle with both arms raised to the square.

John Y. Barlow was administered to for a severe pain in his head. J. Leslie Broadbent anointing and LeGrand Woolley sealing.

Charles F. Zitting offered the closing prayer.

52 B ☙

Minutes of the meeting held Thursday, December 6, 1934.
Place: J. Leslie Broadbent home.
Time: 7:30 p.m.

J. Leslie Broadbent presiding and Joseph W. Musser conducting.
Charles F. Zitting offered the opening prayer.
Sacrament administered by J. Leslie Broadbent and Louis A. Kelsch.
Minutes of the previous meeting read and approved.

J. Leslie Broadbent informed us that Arnold Boss has prepared a history of plural marriage among the Mormons, containing thirty-two chapters. He desires counsel regarding the proper time to publish it.

J. Leslie Broadbent read a synopsis of the book which appears to be a very comprehensive history of Mormon plural marriage.
LeGrand Woolley suggested the history be published as a source book with a minimum of comments, and, if possible, get a prominent publisher such as McMillan, to take his book.
Vote unanimous. (Louis A. Kelsch excused at this point.)

LeGrand Woolley was mouth for the prayer circle – remembering especially, the son of Edmund Barlow who recently met with a serious accident, being shot with a pistol, accidentally. Also petitioned further for a confirmation of our calling.

John Y. Barlow offered the closing prayer.

53 B

Minutes of the meeting held Thursday, December 13, 1934.
Place: J. Leslie Broadbent home.
Time: 7:30 p.m.
J. Leslie Broadbent presiding and Charles F. Zitting conducting.
Opening prayer offered by John Y. Barlow.

Sacrament administered by J. Leslie Broadbent and Louis A. Kelsch.
Minutes of the previous meeting read and approved.

J. Leslie Broadbent presented a case of a woman who has been married about three years, the past two of which, her husband has deserted her. The woman cannot afford a divorce and the husband isn't concerned about it. The woman is now favorable to plural marriage, to another man. What should she do was the question raised.
Considered advisable to get a divorce even if the prospective husband has to help her obtain it with his own finances.
John Y. Barlow moved that such be the advice.
Vote unanimous.

Brother Arnold Boss met with us this evening and gave us an account of what inspired his book and what it consists of. He has, for several years past, gathered valuable material which might very well be published to the world at this time. The work bears strong testimony to the truthfulness and propriety of plural marriage.
Joseph W. Musser moved that Charles F. Zitting get what information he could concerning statements made by Winston Churchill and Dr. Johnson, head of the Eugenics Society of America, with respect to plural marriage among the Mormons, for use in the book.
Vote unanimous.

J. Leslie Broadbent counseled Arnold Boss to work with Joseph W. Musser in arranging and preparing his book. Through this means, the Council will be able to lend their support to this book which will be invaluable as a defense of the truth.
J. Leslie Broadbent moved that the Council set Arnold Boss apart to proceed with his labor.
Vote unanimous.
Joseph W. Musser as mouth in setting him apart.

The prayer circle was dispensed with tonight.
LeGrand Woolley absent by excuse.
Joseph W. Musser closed with prayer.

54 B

Minutes of the meeting held Thursday, December 20, 1934.
Place: J. Leslie Broadbent home.
Time: 7:30 p.m.
J. Leslie Broadbent presiding and Louis A. Kelsch conducting.
Opening prayer offered by Charles F. Zitting.
Sacrament administered by Joseph W. Musser and John Y. Barlow.
Minutes of the previous meetings read and approved.

Commenced study of Section 27, D&C.

LeGrand Woolley came in at this point. Tardiness excused.

Concluded Section 27 and 28.

LeGrand Woolley read an article in the magazine "Time," December 17, 1934 issue, giving an account of the organization of the first L.D.S. stake in New York. Written in a very belittling manner.

J. Leslie Broadbent was mouth for the prayer circle.

LeGrand Woolley moved, that due to the Xmas holidays, we postpone our next meeting until a week next Thursday. Vote unanimous.

LeGrand Woolley closed with prayer, remembering especially Br. Willie Woolley Wardrop, who was seriously injured this evening in an automobile accident.

1935

55 B ☙

Minutes of the meeting held Thursday, January 3, 1935.
Place: J. Leslie Broadbent home.
Time: 7:30 p.m.
J. Leslie Broadbent presiding and conducting.
Charles F. Zitting offered the opening prayer.
Sacrament administered by Louis A. Kelsch and Joseph W. Musser.
Minutes of the previous meeting read and approved.

J. Leslie Broadbent informed us that C. Gustafson was here seeking counsel regarding his moving to Salt Lake City. He decided to move here. He also desires his priesthood ordination made sure.
Charles F. Zitting moved that J. Leslie Broadbent tend to that matter for him.
Vote unanimous.
Many are beginning to realize that the Lord holds a tighter rein on his priesthood than they have heretofore understood and for that reason are seeking to make their priesthood sure.

Charles F. Zitting presented a problem to the Council concerning the Stokes family. After due consideration, Charles F. Zitting moved that the matter be deferred indefinitely but that the matter be referred to again at such time as he feels impressed to bring it before the Council, it being understood that in due time, the matter will be settled.
Vote unanimous.

Louis A. Kelsch was mouth for the prayer circle, remembering especially Sister Margaret Boss who is suffering from pneumonia.

John Y. Barlow and LeGrand Woolley were absent by excuse.

J. Leslie Broadbent closed with prayer

56 B ∽

Minutes of the meeting held Thursday, January 10, 1935.
Place: J. Leslie Broadbent home.
Time: 8:00 p.m.
J. Leslie Broadbent presiding and John Y. Barlow conducting.
Louis A. Kelsch opened with prayer.
Sacrament administered by J. Leslie Broadbent and Joseph W. Musser.
Minutes of the previous meeting read and approved.
LeGrand Woolley absent by excuse.

The Meeting time, for tonight, has been changed from 7:30 to 8:00 p.m. to accommodate John Y. Barlow changed working hours.

Louis A. Kelsch was administered to for a physical ailment, John Y. Barlow anointing and J. Leslie Broadbent sealing.
J. Leslie Broadbent was administered to for a cold and weakness which has been trying to gain a hold upon him, Charles F. Zitting anointing and Joseph W. Musser sealing.

J. Leslie Broadbent informed us that Carl Jentzsch desires his home dedicated.
Joseph W. Musser moved that we leave it to Carl Jentzsch as to whom he desires to invite to his home for the dedication, not having it open to a general gathering.
Vote unanimous.

Brother M. Brown told J. Leslie Broadbent the other day that he sustains us in the priesthood. He then told J. Leslie Broadbent he desired to be advanced in the priesthood.
Joseph W. Musser moved that the matter rest as it is now, providing his present ordination to that of an Elder is proper.

Joseph W. Musser informed us that he has heard that Brother Abraham Teerlink, who has turned against us, appears to be in danger of losing his mind.

J. Leslie Broadbent read a letter to Eslie Jenson from Melvin J. Ballard answering some points mentioned on plural marriage. He acknowledges, among other things, the existence of a revelation in John Taylor's handwriting of 1886.

Louis A. Kelsch was excused at this point.

Charles F. Zitting was mouth in the prayer circle, praying for a speedy confirmation.

John Y. Barlow expressed the feeling that we should spend time in thought and meditation after our Circle prayer instead of rushing to dismiss [. . . .][1]

57 B

Minutes of the meeting held Thursday, January 17, 1935.
Place: J. Leslie Broadbent home.
Time: 8:00 p.m.
J. Leslie Broadbent presiding and Joseph W. Musser conducting.
Louis A. Kelsch offered the opening prayer.
Sacrament administered by Charles F. Zitting and John Y. Barlow.
Minutes of the previous meeting read and approved.

Charles F. Zitting moved that the meetings start at 7:00 p.m. until further notice, that Louis A. Kelsch may be present.

1 The remaining portion of these minutes in the editor's copy of the manuscript is illegible.

J. Leslie Broadbent and John Y. Barlow were appointed to be at Charles Jentzsch home dedication next Sunday evening to represent the Council.

Louis A. Kelsch has an offer to play six nights a week in an orchestra.
The Council feels it wise to play with this orchestra as long as all goes well.

LeGrand Woolley moved that the prayer circle be the first order of business after the minutes.
Vote unanimous.

J. Leslie Broadbent was mouth for the prayer circle this evening.
Louis A. Kelsch excused.
Took up the 29th Section, D&C. Studied to verse 22.
LeGrand Woolley closed with prayer.

58 B

Minutes of the meeting held Thursday, January 24, 1935.
Place: J. Leslie Broadbent home.
Time: 7:00 p.m.
J. Leslie Broadbent presiding and Charles F. Zitting conducting.
Louis A. Kelsch opened with prayer.
Sacrament administered by J. Leslie Broadbent and John Y. Barlow.
Minutes of the previous meeting read and approved.

Joseph W. Musser, as mouth for the prayer circle, asked that J. Leslie Broadbent, who has been ailing in health of late, be strengthened and given a knowledge of the truth.

LeGrand Woolley came in, excused.

J. Leslie Broadbent informed us that Nathaniel Baldwin has asked to have his home dedicated. After due consideration Joseph W. Musser moved that the case be left in J. Leslie Broadbent hands, it being deemed wise to wait a little while before such a dedication.

John Y. Barlow presented the case of Del Pace.
Joseph W. Musser moved that John Y. Barlow take charge of the situation.
Vote unanimous.

Joseph W. Musser told of O. Toomey problem, concerning relief work. J. McKnight has been engaged to represent the case and has asked for a little financial support.
J. Leslie Broadbent moved that we take $10 from the treasury for a start with the proceedings.
Vote unanimous.

Joseph W. Musser and J. Leslie Broadbent have a new work prepared treating a correspondence between Melvin J. Ballard and Eslie Jenson, also being an interpretation of Section 132 D&C. It is hoped it will do much to stop the unrighteous interpretation placed upon it (Section 132) by Melvin J. Ballard and other authorities.

We are to meet next Sunday at 10:00 a.m. at J. Leslie Broadbent home, to read and discuss the work before it goes to the printer.

LeGrand Woolley and Louis A. Kelsch were excused.

Resolved that we prepare a form letter to be sent to those in harmony, soliciting funds to assist in printing.

Balance of Section 29 was read and discussed.
John Y. Barlow offered the closing prayer.

59 B

Minutes of the special meeting held Sunday, January 27, 1935,
at J. Leslie Broadbent home, to read the manuscript.
Time: 10:25 a.m.
J. Leslie Broadbent presiding and conducting.
LeGrand Woolley opened with prayer.

J. Leslie Broadbent and Joseph W. Musser read the manuscript.
LeGrand Woolley moved that with the striking out of two particular paragraphs the work be published as read.
Vote unanimous.

J. Leslie Broadbent read a form letter prepared to be sent to those who are in harmony, soliciting their financial assistance in the printing and mailing of the proposed new booklet.

John Y. Barlow closed with prayer.

60 B

Minutes of the meeting held Thursday, January 31, 1935.
Place: J. Leslie Broadbent home.
J. Leslie Broadbent presiding and LeGrand Woolley conducting.
Time: 7:00 p.m.
Joseph W. Musser opened with prayer.
Sacrament administered by John Y. Barlow and Charles F. Zitting.
Minutes of the previous meeting read and approved.

Joseph W. Musser read some additional matter for use in the new booklet with reference especially to James E. Talmage and the proceedings of a church conference in 1852, at which

the revelation Section 132 was presented to the church and adopted.[2]
J. Leslie Broadbent moved that the material, with some little exception, be incorporated in the new work.
Vote unanimous.

Discussed round dances.

J. Leslie Broadbent recommended that Arthur Halliday be ordained an Elder.
Joseph W. Musser moved that J. Leslie Broadbent take care of the matter.
Vote unanimous.
J. Leslie Broadbent appointed Louis A. Kelsch to take care of the ordination.

Studied Sections 30, 31, D&C.
Charles F. Zitting dismissed.

61 B

Minutes of the meeting held Thursday, February 7, 1935.
Place: J. Leslie Broadbent home.
Time: 7:00 p.m.
J. Leslie Broadbent presiding and Louis A. Kelsch conducting.
J. Leslie Broadbent opened with prayer.
Sacrament administered by Joseph W. Musser and Charles F. Zitting.
Minutes of the previous meeting read and approved.

Joseph W. Musser was mouth for the prayer circle.

LeGrand Woolley came in, tardiness excused.

---

[2] Orson Pratt gave the talk; it is found in *JD* 1:53

J. Leslie Broadbent read a proposed letter from Eslie Jenson to Melvin J. Ballard closing their correspondence on plural marriage.

J. Leslie Broadbent spoke of oneness of mind and the stir it is causing.

Louis A. Kelsch excused.
Studied Sections 32, 33, and 34, D&C.
LeGrand Woolley dismissed.

62 B ☙

Minutes of the meeting held Thursday, February 14, 1935.
Place: J. Leslie Broadbent home.
Time 7:00 p.m.
J. Leslie Broadbent presiding and conducting.
Charles F. Zitting opened with prayer.
Sacrament administered by J. Leslie Broadbent and John Y. Barlow.
Minutes of the previous meeting read and approved.

Louis A. Kelsch was mouth for the prayer circle.

John Y. Barlow and LeGrand Woolley absent by excuse.

Charles F. Zitting appointed to see O. Toomey and encourage him to be dependent upon the Lord to win his case against the state and not to be too sure of himself.

Studied Sections 35, 36, and 37, D&C.
Louis A. Kelsch excused before study.
J. Leslie Broadbent dismissed.

63 B

Minutes of the meeting held Thursday, February 21, 1935.
Place: J. Leslie Broadbent home.
Time 7:00 p.m.
J. Leslie Broadbent presiding and John Y. Barlow conducting.
Charles F. Zitting opened with prayer.
Sacrament administered by J. Leslie Broadbent and Louis A. Kelsch.
Minutes of the previous meeting read and approved.

LeGrand Woolley was mouth for the prayer circle.

Charles F. Zitting reports seeing O. Toomey and that he seemed humble and dependent upon the Lord.

J. Leslie Broadbent reports the new booklet is well on its way and that it will be considerably larger than anticipated and will cost approximately $320 for printing.

After three days in Judge James McKinney's third district court, O. Toomey was found guilty by a jury of eight men of failure to provide for his family. The trial was apparently prejudiced against him from the start and he is in truth, not guilty. The case was, as the paper stated, a trial case between relief agencies and recipients. The real question was – can the relief officials force men on relief rolls to do their will and bidding regardless of the kind of labor and wages offered them. Joseph McKnight was attorney for the defense and Barnell Black, attorney for the state.

J. Leslie Broadbent read a paragraph from an article in Harpers Magazine for March 1935, presaging a revolution in the United States.

Charles F. Zitting moved that we dispense with the lesson tonight, that J. Leslie Broadbent and John Y. Barlow may finish checking the proofs for the new booklet, this evening.

Joseph W. Musser dismissed.

64 B ☙

Minutes of the meeting held Thursday, February 28, 1935.
Place: J. Leslie Broadbent home.
Time: 7:00 p.m.
J. Leslie Broadbent presiding and Joseph W. Musser conducting.
Louis A. Kelsch offered the opening prayer.
Sacrament was administered by John Y. Barlow and LeGrand Woolley.
Minutes of the previous meeting read and approved.

J. Leslie Broadbent as mouth for the prayer circle, pledged our own blood and lives if necessary to help redeem the Saints and reinstate them before the Lord. Also mentioning the apostate condition of the posterity of the former leaders of the Church and Kingdom.

J. Leslie Broadbent gave a bit of history he obtained from O. Toomey from history of early Saints by Bishop George Miller. Fifty Princes of Kingdom mentioned, Joseph to run for President of the United States, etc., showing clearly the early attempt to actually establish the Kingdom of God.

Studied Section 38, D&C.
Charles F. Zitting closed with prayer.

65 B ☙

Minutes of the meeting held Thursday, March 7, 1935.
Place: J. Leslie Broadbent home.
J. Leslie Broadbent presiding and Charles F. Zitting conducting.

Time: 7:00 p.m.
Opening prayer offered by John Y. Barlow.
Sacrament administered by J. Leslie Broadbent and Louis A. Kelsch.
Minutes of the previous meeting read and approved.

Joseph W. Musser read an item from the Deseret News Magazine Section of March 2, 1935 being a letter from Brigham Young to Dr. John M. Bernhisel.

J. Leslie Broadbent read a proposed stated amendment before the present legislature, making cohabitation a felony instead of a misdemeanor and providing that all persons other than the defendant may be compelled to testify. The bill is known as House Bill 224.

J. Leslie Broadbent as mouth for the prayer circle renewed our pledge of last week and in conjunction with our Father in Heaven, cursed those who seek to hinder the Kingdom of God and its advancement, both those in the Church and those out of it.

J. Leslie Broadbent reports the printer has been paid $150.00, leaving a balance of $115.00 in the treasury. Received the first copies of the book today. The cost of mailing is 2 cents a copy.

Proceeded to study and discuss the Fifth Lecture on Faith, with particular reference to the personality of the Father and the Son, one being a personage of Spirit and the other a personage of flesh and bone. Also the personality of the Holy Ghost. Reading from JD 5:179 – Heber C. Kimball – indicating the Holy Ghost to be a Son of God, standing next to Christ. The brethren were cautioned not to advance opinions on these matters before confirming them by the word of the Lord.[3]

---

3 This entry is interesting because, as noted above, many fundamentalists believe that Joseph Smith was the Holy Ghost previous to his probation. If accepted as

Also studied D&C Sections 39, 40, 41.
LeGrand Woolley closed with prayer.

66 B ☙

Minutes of the meeting held Thursday, March 14, 1935.
Place: Louis A. Kelsch's home.
Time: 7:00 p.m.
John Y. Barlow presiding and LeGrand Woolley conducting.
Opening prayer offered by John Y. Barlow.
Sacrament administered by Charles F. Zitting and Joseph W. Musser.
Minutes of the previous meeting read and approved.

Louis A. Kelsch as mouth for the prayer circle, asked the Lord's blessings upon J. Leslie Broadbent who is ill with Bronchial pneumonia.

Joseph W. Musser read a letter from Melvin J. Ballard to Eslie Jenson expressing his disappointment at Eslie Jenson's use of his letters, although he was early informed that they would be used publicly.
Joseph W. Musser moved that the new book be held until after conference and that an extra effort be made to have them paid for by then.
Vote unanimous.

Dispensed with study tonight to visit J. Leslie Broadbent and administer to him.
John Y. Barlow dismissed.

---

true, this entry from the Journal of Discourses places Joseph Smith next to Christ in his seniority over this earth. It seems likely that it was this connection that the council was discussing – and it was this issue that they were likely determining should not be promoted without a witness from the Lord. cf. *D&C* 135:3.

67 B

Minutes of the meeting held Thursday, March 21, 1935.
Place: J. Leslie Broadbent home.
Time: 7:00 p.m.
John Y. Barlow presiding and Louis A. Kelsch conducting.
John Y. Barlow opened the meeting with prayer.
Sacrament administered by LeGrand Woolley and Charles F. Zitting.
Minutes of the previous meeting read and approved.

Joseph W. Musser was mouth for the prayer circle.

Leslie was administered to by his friends last Thursday after meeting. He felt somewhat improved immediately thereafter and although he spent a restless night, seemed to be holding his own.
Friday afternoon Joseph Musser, Lyman Jessop, Arnold Boss, and Louis Kelsch visited with and administered to him and he appeared encouragingly improved. Later in the afternoon, Carl Jentzsch came and visited with him, Louis also being present. When Carl left, Leslie said he felt he had overdone himself a little and wanted to rest.
Dr. Woolley came before 7:00 p.m. and remained about three hours doing all in his power to make Leslie comfortable and well. Rula Broadbent phoned Joseph to come about 10:45 p.m. Carl Jentzsch, at Rula's request, brought John Barlow about 11:00 p.m. These three brethren, with Leslie's and part of Louis' family, then knelt around the bed and each, in turn, offered a prayer in Leslie's behalf. Louis came about 1:30 a.m. and soon Dr. Woolley returned saying he felt too uneasy to stay away longer. Leslie had been given a sleeping medicine about 12:30 a.m. and had gone to sleep. After the Dr. came, they (Dr. and Rula) tried to arouse him to give him oxygen but failed to do so. His breathing and pulse grew steadily weaker and in spite of all that could be done, both spiritually and physically, he passed quietly and peacefully

away at 2:53 a.m. [on March15, 1935]. All the above named, excepting Carl Jentzsch were at the bedside at his passing.

Louis A. Kelsch presented the case of P. Dyre.
John Y. Barlow moved that Joseph W. Musser [sic] explain the situation to her and report back. Vote unanimous.

Louis A. Kelsch reports the book paid for and all copies received.
Discussed the correspondence in the book, Joseph W. Musser reading a proposed answer from Eslie Jenson to Melvin J. Ballard. Joseph W. Musser also read a letter from Rhea Kunz expressing her[4] sincere empathy for those who are grieved over Leslie's passing.
Charles F. Zitting moved that Joseph W. Musser write a form letter to send to some of the uninformed brethren of Leslie's demise. Vote unanimous.

Charles F. Zitting gave an account of the commotion caused by the passing, by this last state legislature, of a law which makes unlawful cohabitation a felony.

John Y. Barlow recommended we have the brethren holding the Patriarchal Priesthood[5] meet each week in a group and combine their prayers with our own, partake of the sacrament and study the scriptures. Let it be known as a "study group," not in any sense to draw away from the Church, but rather to strengthen the hands of the Priesthood.
Moved by Joseph W. Musser. Vote unanimous.

---

4 The original minutes say "his sincere empathy." This could indicate that the handwritten notes incorrectly attribute the letter to Rhea when it should have been attributed to Morris Kunz or it could indicate that the scrivener made a simple error or it could indicate that the usage of "his" was intended to strengthen the code then in usage. The editor has opted for either of the latter interpretations - admittedly, the decision was somewhat arbitrary as each of these positions has merit.

5 This usage of the term "patriarchal priesthood" is helpful because there does not appear to be any suggestion that the term refers to the office of the presiding patriarch as the *Minutes* at 4a suggest. Although it could be a reference to men who were plurally married, it seems more likely that this is referring to men who had received their second anointing.

Decided price of the books be thirty-five cents for white and fifty cents for green cover.

It was decided to invite the brethren and sisters to fast and pray for defeat of the anti-polygamy law, Sunday next, holding a meeting at 7:00 p.m. at Louis A. Kelsch home. The fast to end then.

John Y. Barlow moved that LeGrand Woolley serve as the class leader. Vote unanimous.

LeGrand Woolley closed with prayer.

68 B

Minutes of the meeting held Thursday, March 28, 1935.
Place: J. Leslie Broadbent home.
Time: 7:30 p.m.
John Y. Barlow presiding and conducting.
Charles F. Zitting opened with prayer.
Sacrament administered by Joseph W. Musser and Louis A. Kelsch.
Minutes of the previous meeting read and approved.

John Y. Barlow moved that the following be included in the minutes:
Joseph Reported:
He had been reliably informed that the recent law aimed at those living in polygamy, declaring Unlawful Co-habitation to be a felony and otherwise adding teeth to the measure, was prepared by Hugh B. Brown, President of the Granite Stake and that it was presented to and approved by the High Council of that Stake before it was introduced in the Legislature. It was this Stake that took action against the fellowship of Elders Joseph Leslie Broadbent, Joseph W. Musser, Charles F. Zitting, Louis A. Kelsch et al, because of

their sustaining, in their teachings, the principle of Patriarchal marriage as revealed to the Prophet Joseph Smith.

At the conference session of the above Stake, held March 24, 1935, it is reported, President Brown announced the new law which he explained had been prepared to enable the prosecution of new polygamy cases and that from now on such prosecutions would be vigorous; and that such course had been approved by the Presidency of the Church.
Thus the issue is sharply defined. An apostate Priesthood against God and the laws of Heaven. We shall see what happens to the traducers of righteousness!
Motion [to include the minutes] voted unanimous.

Charles F. Zitting suggested that we follow the plan offered by J. Leslie Broadbent several months ago, to pray for an understanding with the leaders of the Church. That we might be able to reason together.

Charles F. Zitting was mouth in the prayer circle, calling the Lord's attention to the laws being passed against Patriarchal marriage.
Joseph W. Musser read two letters from Byron Harvey Allred in answer to his circular letter informing them of J. Leslie Broadbent's demise; one offering condolences to those bereaved and the other relating two dreams he has had, showing the faithful Saints fleeing from the laws of the land and persecution because of their belief in the fullness of the Gospel.

Joseph W. Musser then read another letter from Price W. Johnson expressing the sorrow of the Saints in their vicinity at hearing of Leslie's passing. Also one from Rhea Kunz sending greeting and good wishes.
Eleven names of brethren were suggested to meet each Thursday and to hold a study class and unite their faith and prayers with the Council for deliverance from Spiritual and financial bondage. The names are:

Albert Barlow Arnold Boss Morris Kunz
Byron Harvey Allred O. Brainich Carl Jentzsch
Lyman Jessop Daniel Bateman George Woodruff
Edmund Lanthus Bert[6]

Joseph W. Musser moved that we meet conjointly with them next Thursday at 744 East South Temple.
Unanimous vote.

Joseph W. Musser moved that Arnold Boss be appointed Secretary of the study class and to give us an account of the minutes each week. Vote unanimous.

John Y. Barlow read from the JD 1:112[7] by Brigham Young on who are worthy of wives.

Joseph W. Musser recounted his experience in the Atlas office with Roy Wilson. Also Roy's reaction the next day.

Louis A. Kelsch closed with prayer.

69 B

Minutes of the meeting held Thursday, April 11, 1935.

---

6 In the original manuscript, only nine names are listed in code. An additional name, Edmund Lanthus Bert, was penciled in when the other code names were deciphered.

7 The talk begins on page 112 but the subject alluded to does not appear until page 119. In summary, Brigham Young commented that before a man asked his permission to receive a wife, the man should first honor his priesthood and magnify his calling. Then, he should prove his integrity and righteousness to keep the wife in eternity. The reader may note that in Brigham Young's day, men approached the man holding the sealing keys to request permission to be sealed to someone and they approached him to request permission to court the woman as well.

Place: J. Leslie Broadbent home.
Time: 7:30 p.m.
John Y. Barlow presiding and Joseph W. Musser conducting.
Louis A. Kelsch opened with prayer.
Sacrament administered by John Y. Barlow and Charles F. Zitting.
Minutes of the previous meeting read and approved.

John Y. Barlow as mouth for the prayer circle, called the Lord's attention to the pitfall prepared by the Church leaders to ensnare us and of Lorin C. Woolley's prophecy in 1922 that they might try to imprison us for living the Patriarchal order of marriage but that the one mighty and strong would not let them do it.

Joseph W. Musser informed us that J. Whitaker told sister A. Pettit that committees had been formed in the stakes and wards for the purpose of getting information to be used against the polygamists in the attempt to put them [in] prison. Also that Mac. Barlow's lady friend told him that her mother (who works in the County Attorney's office) had helped prepare warrants for the arrest of many of those suspected of having more than one wife.

LeGrand Woolley read an editorial from the "Saints Herald," March 26, 1935 issue (Reorganites) on the new law passed against Patriarchal Marriage in the last Utah Legislature.

Joseph W. Musser read a letter from Price W. Johnson asserting his, and others, allegiance to the cause in which we are engaged. They plan to raise a large crop of various foodstuffs to do their part in preparing for the famine which is upon us.

Discussed making a trip to Southern Utah and Northern Arizona to visit some of the Saints.

Joseph W. Musser read some interesting extracts of sermons of former Church leaders on the judgments to befall us in these last days if we did not turn unto the Lord. And the Mormons have forsaken the Lord. The judgments foretold are now hanging over our heads and are in the process of fulfillment. Each day sees the literal fulfillment of those prophecies. And those are but the beginning of sorrows among the Mormons.

Discussed holding meetings with the Saints. How often and where? The attendance at cottage meetings is increasing until it will soon be necessary to find a hall or some such place in order to accommodate those who are starving and searching after the truth.

Charles F. Zitting was appointed to get a detailed account of the Church indebtedness.

Joseph W. Musser offered the closing prayer.

70 B

Minutes of the meeting held Thursday, April 25, 1935.
Place: J. Leslie Broadbent home.
Time: 7:30 p.m.
John Y. Barlow presiding and Joseph W. Musser conducting.
Opening prayer offered by John Y. Barlow.
Sacrament administered by Charles F. Zitting and LeGrand Woolley.

LeGrand Woolley was mouth for the prayer circle.
Joseph W. Musser read a letter of protest addressed to Heber J. Grant, protesting against his public statements characterizing polygamous families as "illegitimate" and born of "passion" only. The same was approved, Joseph W. Musser assuming the responsibility personally by attaching his name.

Joseph W. Musser's request that he be permitted to begin the publication of a magazine to be called TRUTH for the sole purpose of disseminating the Gospel, was approved.

A trip into Southern Utah and Northern Arizona by John Y. Barlow and Joseph W. Musser (for the purpose of meeting and counseling with the brethren there) was approved.

Louis A. Kelsch was absent by excuse.
Joseph W. Musser closed with prayer.

71 B

Minutes of the meeting held Thursday, May 9, 1935.
Place: J. Leslie Broadbent home.
Time: 7:30 p.m.
John Y. Barlow presiding and Charles F. Zitting conducting.
Louis A. Kelsch opened with prayer.
Sacrament administered by John Y. Barlow and Charles F. Zitting.
Minutes of the previous meeting read and approved.

Joseph W. Musser as mouth for the prayer circle offered a most inspired, comprehensive prayer for the imperiled saints and those who seek to advance the Kingdom of God. Asked the Lord to confound our enemies, ensnaring them in the pit they have laid for the faithful. Remembered especially Sister Anne Jessop who is suffering from a stroke.

Joseph W. Musser gave an account of the trip south. Organized a study circle in Short Creek.

Joseph W. Musser read a letter from Price W. Johnson of Short Creek asking for three men to help with their crops and in the lumber mill, thereby opening the way to establish the families of the three men in Short Creek.

After due consideration of eligible brethren Joseph W. Musser moved that the following brethren be sent south in answer to the invitation:

Albert Barlow
Lyman Jessop
Carl Jentzsch
Vote unanimous.

John Y. Barlow felt that several of the brethren should be advanced in the Priesthood to the office of High Priest. Joseph W. Musser moved John Y. Barlow be authorized to ordain those of the brethren whom he feels are prepared. Vote unanimous.

Joseph W. Musser presented the case of George Woodruff who desires to be administered to regularly for the restoration of his sight. Felt best to abide our time and not be too insistent upon the Lord nor to make the administration for the sick too commonplace.

John Y. Barlow spoke of the situation in Millville where more brethren were invited to the study group than were selected to attend.

Joseph W. Musser read a note from 728DR9" pledging $1.00 a month for the rest of his life for the promulgation of the truth. Exhibited a fine spirit.

John Y. Barlow closed with prayer.

72 B

Minutes of the meeting held Thursday, May 16, 1935.
Place: J. Leslie Broadbent home.
Time: 7:30 p.m.

John Y. Barlow presided and Louis A. Kelsch conducted.
Joseph W. Musser opened with prayer.
Sacrament administered by John Y. Barlow and Louis A. Kelsch.
Minutes of the previous meeting read and approved.

John Y. Barlow as mouth for the prayer circle asked especially for help for the council by having more men added to our numbers.

LeGrand Woolley informed us that A5J8F"91 was operated on last midnight. He is in a very serious condition having about a twenty-five percent chance of recovery. Infection has been poisoning his system for several hours.

Discussed the "Open Letter" and other present day perplexities.

Joseph W. Musser presented 8DQ3"15 case regarding his priesthood.
John Y. Barlow moved Joseph W. Musser attend to the matter.
Joseph W. Musser asked what should be our attitude where good wives have been left widows through their husband's death.
Understanding is that widows should not remarry except under the order of the Priesthood.
The scriptures say the brother should take them.

Charles F. Zitting absent by excuse.
LeGrand Woolley closed.

73 B

Minutes of the meeting held June 13, 1935.
Place: 744 East South Temple.
Time: 9:00 a.m.

John Y. Barlow presiding and conducting.
Louis A. Kelsch opened with prayer.
Sacrament administered by Joseph W. Musser and John Y. Barlow.
Minutes of the previous meeting read and approved.

John Y. Barlow spoke of the possibilities in the south for the Saints. Also the relief officials threaten to cut off the relief of families where a work card has been sent to the man and he has been unable to answer due to being out of town working to prepare a way to get his families off the relief rolls.
LeGrand Woolley felt it unwise to attempt too big a proposition in the south because of the natural lack of that section of country, feeling that its possibilities are very limited.

Several brethren, both south and locally have expressed their desire of turning over to the Priesthood all their earthly possessions. The spirit of the United Order is prevailing upon them heavily and that without our solicitation.
Joseph W. Musser explained briefly a "Service Exchange" system presented by Q379F5. The plan, it appears, would be a fine system to prepare the Saints for the United Order.
Discussed at considerable length the different phases of the economic plan which has loomed up before us within the last two months. The spirit of most of the Saints has turned toward this new economic endeavor.

Joseph W. Musser moved John Y. Barlow return to Short Creek and supervise the efforts there with a view to developing an organization adequate to handle any properties that may be tendered and that consideration to such organization be given by us brethren.
Vote unanimous.

Charles F. Zitting absent by excuse.

LeGrand Woolley, as mouth for the prayer circle, thanks the Lord for His direction and the manifestation of His Spirit and asked a continuance of the same. Also closed the meeting.

74 B

Minutes of the meeting held Thursday, June 27, 1935.
Place: 744 East South Temple.
Time: 9:00 a.m.
John Y. Barlow presided and Joseph W. Musser conducted.
Charles F. Zitting opened with prayer.
Sacrament administered by Louis A. Kelsch and Joseph W. Musser.
Minutes of the previous meeting read and approved.

John Y. Barlow was mouth for the prayer circle.

LeGrand Woolley excused.

Louis A. Kelsch read a letter from Short Creek showing some discord among the brethren there. Read minutes of two of their meetings.
Charles F. Zitting moved a letter of acknowledgement be sent to Short Creek informing them that John Y. Barlow was coming down soon.
Vote unanimous.

Joseph W. Musser counseled us to be wise in our counsel and to strive to set ourselves in order, which we must do, before we can attempt to teach others.

Note – The "United Trust" was organized on June 26, 1935, with John Y. Barlow, Joseph W. Musser and Charles F. Zitting as Trustees, taking in the forty-acre farm of C. H. Owen, forty-acre farm of C. F. Zitting and 2,800 shares of Senrab Oil Stock from E. F. Barlow.

Upon the motion of John Y. Barlow, Louis Kelsch was recommended as a trustee in the "United Trust." Vote was unanimous.

Joseph W. Musser informed us the second number of "Truth" will be out today.

John Y. Barlow said that stopping of relief has been threatened for the DC95"3G family unless he comes back to town and answers his work cards.[8]
Thought best to keep him where he is for the present.

Discussed several items of current interest.

Joseph W. Musser closed with prayer.

75 B

Minutes of the meeting held July 11, 1935.
Place: South Temple.
Time: 9:00 a.m.
Joseph W. Musser presiding as John Y. Barlow is in Short Creek, Arizona. Charles F. Zitting conducted.
LeGrand Woolley opened with prayer.
Sacrament administered by Joseph W. Musser and Louis A. Kelsch.
Minutes of the previous meeting read and approved.

Joseph W. Musser, as mouth for the prayer circle, prayed for moisture for the crops at Short Creek. Several of the brethren here have united with the Short Creek brethren in a season of fasting to obtain rain.

---

[8] See *Minutes* 73b for background on this issue.

Joseph W. Musser explained the new "Trust" organization to LeGrand Woolley. Thought best to keep his name off the board of trustees at present.

Joseph W. Musser read a letter from Laura Barlow of Short Creek asking for $30.00 to help finish 8FJAK5 home. Charles F. Zitting moved that the matter be presented to a Thursday night meeting and perhaps the funds can be raised. Vote unanimous.

Joseph W. Musser read a letter from Eslie Jenson informing us of the birth of another son and inquiring about having the child blessed, also having his son ordained a deacon. LeGrand Woolley moved to let the ward authorities act and then if not done properly, he should do it himself.
Vote unanimous.

Charles F. Zitting moved we keep a record of all time and money received and spent under our jurisdiction.
Vote unanimous.

Louis A. Kelsch closed.

76 B ☙

Minutes of the meeting held July 19, 1935.
Place: South Temple.
Time: 9:00 a.m.
John Y. Barlow presiding and Louis A. Kelsch conducting.
John Y. Barlow opened with prayer.
Sacrament administered by Joseph W. Musser and Charles F. Zitting.
Minutes of the previous meeting read and approved.

The Short Creek residents received rain on the Sunday following the fast.

$12.00 was received from the brethren and sent to 8FJAK5 to help buy shingles for his home in Short Creek.

John Y. Barlow was mouth for the prayer circle.

At the instance of 1KD8P138, Joseph W. Musser raised the question as to what should be done with her earthly possessions, to whom to deed them, etc. In short, what would be best for her to [do] with them for the best of all concerned.
It was the united feeling that she deed her possessions to the United Trust subject to a life estate in herself.

Charles F. Zitting moved that we create a Priesthood Library and that we invite contributions of books and other properties to it and on receiving books, that we write the inscription of such book "Property of the Priesthood Library, contributed by __________ name __________ and date."
Joseph W. Musser to be Librarian.
Vote unanimous.

LeGrand Woolley closed.

77 B ☙

Minutes of the meeting held August 1, 1935.
Place: South Temple.
Time: 9:00 a.m.
Joseph W. Musser presiding and conducting.
Charles F. Zitting opened.
Sacrament administered by Joseph W. Musser and Louis A. Kelsch.
Minutes of the previous meeting read and approved.

Joseph W. Musser read a letter from John Y. Barlow giving an account of conditions in Short Creek.

Joseph W. Musser as mouth for the prayer circle remembered especially our brethren at Short Creek who, according to reports, are in jeopardy, state officials having threatened them with arrest.

Decided to send literature to some of the state officials both in Southern Utah and Arizona that they might be made acquainted with our position.
Charles F. Zitting moved that Joseph W. Musser write John Y. Barlow for suggestions concerning a sister for washing and anointing of expectant mothers.[9]
Vote unanimous.

Brothers Charles Kingston and C. Gustafson are at this home this a.m. as missionaries, traveling without purse and scrip calling the people to repentance. (They informed us that Elden Kingston couldn't deliver his message at the meeting last Sunday because the spirit of the congregation was not receptive.)

Joseph W. Musser moved that Charles F. Zitting be authorized to use his judgment concerning A. Anderson regarding his ordination to the Priesthood.
Vote unanimous.

Charles F. Zitting moved that we take minutes of our public meetings.
Vote unanimous.

John Y. Barlow in Short Creek.
Louis A. Kelsch closed.

---

9 This ordinance is no longer performed by the LDS Church. See Beecher, Maureen Ursenbach and Anderson, Lavina F., *Sisters in Spirit: Mormon Women in Historical and Cultural Perspective* (University of Illinois Press: 1992), 130-31 (Chapter: Gifts of the Spirit: Women's Share by Linda King Newell) for a description of this ordinance.

78 B

Minutes of the meeting held Thursday, August 8, 1935.
Place: South Temple.
Time: 9:00 a.m.
John Y. Barlow presiding. He arrived from Short Creek night before last.
John Y. Barlow conducting.
Louis A. Kelsch opened.
Sacrament administered by Joseph W. Musser and Charles F. Zitting.
Minutes of the previous meeting read and approved.

It was suggested that I. Barlow be set apart as an official reporter of our public meetings.
Joseph W. Musser moved that anytime that John Y. Barlow calls on any of us we consider it an official calling and go. Vote unanimous.

John Y. Barlow as mouth for the prayer circle asked the Lord to stem the spirit of apostasy and discontent that has crept in among those who are trying to live the fullness of the Gospel.

Joseph W. Musser suggested that we meet with the other group of brethren at E. Barlow's tonight, lay the matter before them, calling those to account and repentance who need it and have a cleanup of this contention and in harmony. If they will not stop their fighting and be united, they will have to stay away from the meetings.

John Y. Barlow said the discontent in Short Creek was due to the brethren that went down from here. The local brethren there are united with us in every respect.

Local officials in Short Creek refused to sign complaints against our brethren.

Discussed several current questions of import.

LeGrand Woolley closed.

79 B

Minutes of the meeting held Thursday, August 15, 1935.
Place: South Temple.
Time: 9:00 a.m.
Joseph W. Musser presided as John Y. Barlow has returned to Short Creek.
Joseph W. Musser conducted.
Louis A. Kelsch opened.
Sacrament administered by Charles F. Zitting and Louis A. Kelsch.
Minutes of the previous meeting read and approved.

Joseph W. Musser read a letter from BQ5G9FQ91 giving a few details of the action of the law in Short Creek. Warrants have been issued for a few of the brethren, the complaint having been signed by Jack Childers. Another letter from G7C3AF53F containing minutes of their last meeting of August 11, 1935 was read. It showed some misunderstandings and dissatisfaction, especially on the part of two of the brethren from here.

Discussed the cloud burst and flood which struck Short Creek the latter part of last week.

Charles F. Zitting was mouth for the prayer circle asking for blessings of unity upon the Short Creek brethren, remembered R3EQ18N who has been reported as being friendly to the polygamists and asked for judgments of fire, both from heaven and gun, upon this world.

Louis A. Kelsch read a message from one George Otis who claims he is God's messenger. He desires our financial support in publishing his message. Felt we were unable to endorse it in any sense, that he must act on his own responsibility entirely. This man tried to deliver a message at a session of the last general conference of the L.D.S. Church but was forcibly ejected from the building before he could do so.

In discussing the wiles and deceptions of Satan which will be manifest more and more in these last days Joseph W. Musser said he will not be able to deceive us fatally.

Charles F. Zitting was asked to write an account of his experiences with R8QD8NJ3F. The account follows these minutes.

A woman named 9RF8Q81"3D" [Edna ?], a neighbor of Louis A. Kelsch, died in a local hospital last Monday night. It was reported that she tried to circulate a petition in her neighborhood to get J. Leslie Broadbent and Louis A. Kelsch forced out of that neighborhood. Her husband said she considered our manner of living a personal affront to her.

LeGrand Woolley absent by excuse.

Joseph W. Musser closed. Remembered the several Allred children in California who desire to come to these valleys to live.

80 B

Minutes of the meeting held Thursday, August 22, 1935.
Place: South Temple.
Time: 9:00 a.m.
Joseph W. Musser presiding and Charles F. Zitting conducting.
Louis A. Kelsch opened.
Sacrament administered by Joseph W. Musser and Charles F. Zitting.

Louis A. Kelsch was mouth for the prayer circle calling for judgments upon the wicked.

Louis A. Kelsch read minutes from Millville and Short Creek. The Short Creek minutes showing a unity obtains again.

LeGrand Woolley read an article on the United Order[10] prepared to be published in the September issue of "Truth." Also the article, "A Tempest In a Tea Pot,"[11] for the same publication of "Truth."

LeGrand Woolley offered the benediction.

81 B ☙

Minutes of the meeting held Thursday, August 29, 1935.
Place: South Temple.
Time: 9:00 a.m.
Joseph W. Musser presiding and Louis A. Kelsch conducting.
Charles F. Zitting offered the opening prayer.
Sacrament administered by Joseph W. Musser and Louis A. Kelsch.
Minutes of the previous meeting read and approved.

Joseph W. Musser was mouth for the prayer circle.

Administered to Lucy Musser for improvement of health. Charles F. Zitting anointing and Joseph W. Musser sealing.

Joseph W. Musser presented the case of Joseph Marston. Charles F. Zitting moved Joseph W. Musser take care of the matter.
Vote unanimous.

---

10 *Truth* 1:41 #4 appears to contain this article. However, an article by Brigham Young on the same topic is found in *Truth* 1:37 #4.
11 *Truth* 1:43 #4.

Joseph W. Musser read a letter from A. W. Morrison including a letter of his (Morrison's) to David A. Smith. Also, Smith's answer.

Charles F. Zitting read an interesting account of Wilford Woodruffs signing of the manifesto. Account follows these minutes.[12]

Discussed items of current interest.

John Y. Barlow absent, being in Short Creek.
LeGrand Woolley dismissed.

82 B

Minutes of the meeting held Thursday, September 19, 1935.
Place: 744 East South Temple
Time: 9:45 a.m.
John Y. Barlow is here from Short Creek but has gone to Ogden and has not, at this time, returned.
Joseph W. Musser presided and conducted.
Charles F. Zitting opened with prayer.
Sacrament was administered by Louis A. Kelsch and LeGrand Woolley.
Minutes of the previous meeting read and approved.

Joseph W. Musser read a letter from Samuel Eastman advocating a convention for those concerned in the new religious spirit which is arising among the Saints.

F. Cleveland offered to move to Ogden to work and also to represent and the better promulgate the truth there. Thought advisable not to attempt such a move now.

[12] Notably and regrettably, this document is missing from the record.

Discussed at considerable length the feasibility of organizations for the excommunicated Saints.

Charles F. Zitting moved that, on account of the isolated condition of the Short Creek Saints and because they are in the majority, that we approve a Sunday School organization for them.
Vote unanimous.

LeGrand Woolley as mouth for the prayer circle asked that the Lord speedily send one mighty and strong to set His house in order.

LeGrand Woolley read a letter to Joseph W. Musser from 5A91E8FD"3NR of Beverly Hills, California voicing his determination to devote his life and talents to the spreading of truth and also asking for a certain number of books each week and volunteering financial assistance each week.

Joseph W. Musser closed with prayer.

83 B ☙

Minutes of the meeting held Thursday, September 26, 1935.
Place: 744 East South Temple
Time: 9:00 a.m.
Joseph W. Musser presiding and Charles F. Zitting conducting.
Joseph W. Musser opened with prayer.
Sacrament was administered by Louis A. Kelsch and LeGrand Woolley.
Minutes of the previous meeting read and approved.

LeGrand Woolley was mouth for the prayer circle.

Louis A. Kelsch read a proposal from S8D"8Q9G9J"N to publish a leaflet at the coming conference of the L.D.S. to expose some of the inconsistencies of the Church leaders. LeGrand Woolley moved that we do not resort to such a publication.
Vote unanimous.

Joseph W. Musser read a letter from S. Lloyd disclaiming any intention to remuneration for his sale of books in California.

Brothers Price W. Johnson, I. W. Carling and Sister Sylvia Allred are on trial Saturday, September 28, in Short Creek for "open and notorious cohabitation." Several are planning on going down from here to attend.

LeGrand Woolley moved Joseph W. Musser attend and choose between I. W. or E. Barlow as to which he feels is best suited to go with him.

Joseph W. Musser informs us that rumor has it there is going to be a change in the L.D.S. garment at the next conference.

LeGrand Woolley raised the question of all kneeling when the Sacrament is being blessed.

Decided to bring it up later when all are present and in the mean time find out what we can on the subject.

John Y. Barlow absent in Short Creek.
Charles F. Zitting closed.

84 B

Minutes of the meeting held Thursday, October 3, 1935.
Place: 744 East South Temple.
Time: 9:00 a.m.

Joseph W. Musser presiding and LeGrand Woolley conducting.
Louis A. Kelsch opened with prayer.
Minutes of the previous meeting were read, some corrections made and approved.
Sacrament was administered by Joseph W. Musser and Charles F. Zitting.

Joseph W. Musser was mouth for the prayer circle.

Joseph W. Musser took Arnold Boss, L. Allred, Athey and 1P138RP9FJ [Broadbent] to Short Creek. The Pathe and Paramount news were there with their picture and sound equipment to record the trial as were the Associated and United Press Correspondents. Court convened at 9:00 a.m. As it was apparent that the Court ruling on a question of law would be against the contention of the prosecution, the County Attorney (E. Elmo Bollinger) moved for a change of venue from Short Creek to Kingman, Arizona, the preliminaries to be held before the Superior Court there. By stipulation between the attorneys, the motion was granted. The defendants continuing at liberty under their bonds and the state arranging to take them to Kingman for the trial at its expense. General meeting was held Saturday night. Sunday morning Sunday School was held at which sixty-nine were present. The meetings were attended with a most beautiful spirit.

The last dollar has been paid on the land and sawmill. During the last twelve months $2,000.00 have been paid off, $1,400.00 in the last four months since we have been connected with them.

Eight tons of produce have been shipped into Short Creek this summer in exchange for their firewood as also several head of livestock.

They lack potatoes, onions, and wheat.

The Washington Post published a very fair article on the Short Creek episode Sunday, September 29, 1935, although it was not entirely accurate. About one hundred column inches were used. Two other articles from the Ogden Standard-Examiner were presented by Charles F. Zitting.

Joseph W. Musser read from President Roosevelt's recent Los Angeles speech in which he said:
"In the United States, we regard it as axiomatic that every person shall enjoy the free exercise of his religion according to the dictates of his conscience. Our flag for a century and a half has been the symbol of the principles of liberty of conscience, of religious freedom and equality before the law; and these concepts are deeply engrained in our national character."

John Y. Barlow was absent in Short Creek.
Charles F. Zitting closed with prayer.

85 B

Minutes of Priesthood Meeting, October 24, 1935.
Taken by Joseph W. Musser.

Present: Joseph W. Musser, Charles F. Zitting, and LeGrand Woolley, the latter conducting.
Opening prayer: Charles F. Zitting.
Sacrament: Joseph W. Musser and LeGrand Woolley.
Joseph W. Musser mouth in payer.

Brother Musser reported his trip to California, from October 12th to 19th. Had met with a number of Saints there, holding one general meeting and several private or informal gatherings. Organized a prayer and study group consisting of six members, Elder Rulon C. Allred in charge.

Francis M. Darter has asked direction or permission of the Priesthood to spend some time lecturing on his books, particularly the "Bible in Stone" and "Zion's Redemption." He is in a position to get a furlough[13] from the Ry. Co. where he is now working and desires to spend the three months or more in this work.
Decided to advise him that he is at liberty to undertake such work on his own responsibility, cautioning him against setting definite dates that cannot be substantiated by the revelations of the Lord; also against making it definite who the "Mighty and Strong" one is until he shall be properly revealed.

Closing prayer Joseph W. Musser.

86 B ☙

Minutes of Priesthood Meeting, October 31, 1935.
Taken by Joseph W. Musser.
Present: Joseph W. Musser, Charles F. Zitting, and LeGrand Woolley.
Joseph presiding and offering opening prayer.
Sacrament administered by Charles and LeGrand.
Minutes of previous meeting read and approved.
Also, minutes of Short Creek meetings, Millville and Los Angeles.

Circle prayer, LeGrand Woolley mouth.

Case of Bert Olson and his responsibility toward the young lady in Sweden to whom he sent transportation to come to America, but she now appears reluctant about coming.
Decided he should consider himself released unless she complied with his requests to immigrate to America at once.

---

13 i.e., a leave of absence.

The question of Ida Jessop being sent to her husband at Short Creek was discussed, and decided to await direction from President Barlow before sending any one down there.

Closing prayer Charles F. Zitting.

87 B ☙

Special Meeting
Minutes of the meeting held Tuesday, November 26, 1935.
Place: 744 East South Temple
Time: 5:00 p.m.
All present.
John Y. Barlow presiding and conducting.
LeGrand Woolley opened with prayer.
Sacrament was administered by Joseph W. Musser and Louis A. Kelsch.
Minutes of the meeting of October 31, 1935 were read and approved.

Joseph W. Musser was mouth for the prayer circle.

Decided to discontinue kneeling during administration of the Sacrament, or rather during the blessing of same.

Joseph W. Musser read a letter from Byron Harvey Allred telling of a questionnaire circulated in his community by the church authorities. To be answered "yes" or "no," in the effort to find out who sustains the church authorities unreservedly and who does not. Shall he accept the invitations of Sectarian ministers to use their pulpits to expose present conditions in the L.D.S. Church? he asks.
Decided he should not accept the invitations.

John Y. Barlow gave an account of the activities in Short Creek. Also the coats and shoes he was able to purchase for the Short Creek Saints, at unheard of bargains, on a recent visit to California. Further, the legal aspects of the trial set for December 9, 1935 at Kingman. The sawmill and six hundred and forty acres of land are paid for and deeds obtained therefore. Shortage was reported on white flour.

Joseph W. Musser read an article from the New York Evening Journal, on the Polygamy question. A very favorable interview between John Y. Barlow and Gordon Gordon, International News Reporter.

Joseph W. Musser sent a letter to President Franklin D. Roosevelt asking him to have the Government relief records in Short Creek kept confidential and not be used as evidence in the coming trial. Dated, November 13, 1935.

Charles F. Zitting closed with prayer.

1936

88 B

Special Meeting.
Minutes of the meeting held Tuesday, January 14, 1936.
Place: 744 East South Temple.
Time: 7:00 p.m.
All present.
John Y. Barlow presiding and conducting.
Louis A. Kelsch opened with prayer.
Sacrament was administered by Charles F. Zitting and LeGrand Woolley.

John Y. Barlow read and presented the names of several committees, a list of which follows these minutes.
Accepted by unanimous vote.

LeGrand Woolley suggested that Joseph W. Musser contact 1QD8753F and perhaps R3EQ18N and solicit church support in financing the fight to establish the unconstitutionality, by Supreme Court of United States decision, of the laws against plural marriage.
Charles F. Zitting moved Joseph W. Musser follow LeGrand Woolley suggestion.
Unanimous vote.

Charles F. Zitting reported, for the financial committee, that $200.00 of the $500.00 necessary to take the Kingman, Arizona case to the state supreme court had been raised and sent to the attorney in Los Angeles.

Louis A. Kelsch reported on the circulation committee and Joseph W. Musser on the co-operative stores committee.
The question was asked, should we join in with other non-religious and non-political co-operative organizations?
Louis A. Kelsch moved we recommend to the committee in charge, that we do not join with any outside co-operative organization in which we could not have full control.

Vote unanimous.

Joseph W. Musser was mouth for the prayer.
LeGrand Woolley closed.

GENERAL COMMITTEES

John Y. Barlow, Gen. Chairman.

FINANCE:
Charles F. Zitting, Chairman.
Heber K. Cleveland, Salt Lake
Kara H. Lindsay, Salt Lake
Eslie D. Jenson, Millville, Utah
Ernest P. Williams, Los Angeles
Elmer Johnson, Short Creek
Carl O. Holm, Idaho Falls

PUBLISHING:
Joseph W. Musser, Chairman
Arnold Boss, Salt Lake
Rulon C. Allred, Long Beach.

CIRCULATION:
Louis A. Kelsch, Chairman.
Lyman Jessop, Salt Lake
Jesse Martin, Salt Lake
William Thomas, Salt Lake
A. L. Cook, Salt Lake
Sherman Lloyd, Los Angeles.
Isaac Carling, Short Creek
Fallace B. Petty, Pocatello
Joseph T. Jones, Rexburg
John T. Bistline, Logan.

CO-OPERATIVE STORES:
Joseph W. Musser, Chairman.

Salt Lake Division:
Charles H. Owen,
Edmund Barlow
Burt Barlow

Other Committees, such as Agricultural, Town sites, Mining, Educational, Recreational, to be provided for as circumstances warrant.

89 B ଓ

Minutes of the meeting held Thursday, January 23, 1936.

Place: South Temple.
Time: 9:00 a.m.
Joseph W. Musser presiding and conducting.
Charles F. Zitting opened with prayer.
Sacrament administered by Louis A. Kelsch and Joseph W. Musser.
Minutes of the previous meeting read and approved.

Charles F. Zitting asked would it be advisable for him to baptize T73"FLK8 daughter on her eighth birthday? T is still in good standing in the church. Yes, as the church rule forbids baptism to children of parents who have lived as T has.

Charles F. Zitting also presented a problem of 7P8DR9" regarding his partaking of the Sacrament. As his wife is not favorable, he may partake of it by himself or with another man's family.

Joseph W. Musser read a letter from Price Johnson, from the State Penitentiary at Florence, Arizona. He asks that friends be wise in writing, as all mail is read by prison authorities, both incoming and outgoing.

Joseph W. Musser read an answering letter from Carl Johnson, son of Price Johnson, showing a very kindly and friendly spirit. Also, Joseph W. Musser's answer to Carl.

Joseph W. Musser read a letter from DG981DQ1BJQAD37 from Pennsylvania. Shows that "Truth" is reaching the honest in heart regardless of distance.

Joseph W. Musser read a letter from Byron Harvey Allred telling briefly of his trial and excommunication from the church by his Stake authorities.
Also, Joseph W. Musser's answer.

Louis A. Kelsch was mouth for the prayer circle.

John Y. Barlow and LeGrand Woolley excused.
Joseph W. Musser closed.

90 B

Minutes of the meeting held Thursday, February 13, 1936.
Place: South Temple.
Time: 11:00 a.m.
Joseph W. Musser presiding and conducting.
Joseph W. Musser opened with prayer.
Sacrament administered by Charles F. Zitting and Louis A. Kelsch.
Minutes of the previous meeting read and approved.

Hereafter, until further notice, the Council will meet at 11:00 a.m. instead of 9:00 a.m. Thursdays.

It was agreed to publish, in the next "Truth," a brief account of the recent trial of several Millville Saints before their local Church authorities.

Joseph W. Musser read a letter from Brother C. J. Hunt of the Re-organized Church showing a purported refutation of plural marriage by Oliver Cowdery, David Whitmer, Martin Harris and Hyrum Page.

In the Reorganized Saints Herald for February 4, 1936, Elbert A. Smith starts a series of articles on "Differences That Persist in Our Relations With The Utah Mormon Church."

Joseph W. Musser read a letter from Byron Harvey Allred of February 4, 1936 relative to his recent trial, in Idaho, before Church authorities, desiring our advice on appealing his case to higher church courts at the seat of the Church Presidency. Decided to leave the matter in Joseph W. Musser hands.

Joseph W. Musser read from the "Coming Millennium" also an article from Daniel H. Wells, showing that out of the body of Saints in these latter days should evolve a nucleus of the Millennial population.[1]

John Y. Barlow excused.
LeGrand Woolley was mouth for the prayer circle also closing with prayer.

91 B

Minutes of the meeting held Thursday, February 22, 1936.
Place: South Temple.
Time: 11:00 a.m.
John presided and conducted.
Charles opened with prayer.
Minutes of the previous meeting were read and approved.

Joseph read a letter dated February 12, from Attorney Victor J. Hayek, stating that he had heard from what he considered fairly reliable authority that prosecutions were to begin in Salt Lake the latter part of February, similar to the Short Creek proceedings.
John advised that if such a situation arises, certain men had better disappear than risk going to prison.

John informed us on conditions in Short Creek. Not much snow but plenty of rain until the ground is thoroughly soaked. Working on canal. John has an option to buy C. Black's holdings in Short Creek for $1,000.

Brother Byron H. Allred is visiting in town and has just been invited to join and partake of the Sacrament with us.
Sacrament administered by Joseph and Louis.

---

1 There are at least three statements from apostle Daniel H. Wells that could be referred to here: *JD* 16:131-32; 18:96; 23:305-06. For a similar statement from Orson Pratt, see *JD* 15:361.

LeGrand mouth for the prayer circle.

Brother Allred gave a brief account of his trial and excommunication from the Church, as also a report of conditions in that section of the country. He further related a dream he had of following the "Ark of God" over a great plain and of the powerless opposition by Heber J. Grant (whose countenance was darkened with anger and hate).

Joseph read an outline of the appeal of Brother Allred to Heber J. Grant for a retrial before the highest Church tribunal. D&C Sections 102 & 107.
Joseph moved the Council endorse the proposed procedure. Unanimous vote.

John closed with prayer.

92 B

Minutes of the meeting held Tuesday, June 2, 1936.
Place: South Temple.
Time: 9:30 a.m.
John residing and conducting.
Joseph opened with prayer.
Sacrament administered by LeGrand and Louis.
All present.

John counseled us to be very careful in giving blessings. We must learn to say no as well as yes. We are taking a great responsibility upon us and must use the greatest wisdom in these matters. Go to the Lord and seek his spirit for discernment.

John told us some of his remarkable experiences in seeing those who have passed beyond, especially John and Lorin

Woolley. We were also given a brief account of what has been accomplished, as well as the possibilities at Short Creek.

Joseph reported Mr. Hayek as saying the articles of the United Trust were good and sufficient. The proposed lease agreement between the United Trust, Lessor, and the Lessee, was read. With a non-transferable clause added, the lease was unanimously accepted.

John mouth for the prayer circle.

Charles closed.

93 B

Minutes of Council meeting held September 13, 1936.
Present: John Y. Barlow, Joseph W. Musser, Charles F. Zitting, and LeGrand Woolley.
Joseph W. Musser offered prayer.
Sacrament administered by Charles F. Zitting and LeGrand Woolley.

The main business of the meeting being to adjust the affairs of the Saints at Short Creek. Elder Barlow proceeded to outline the condition of the Saints there and of the work; first asking that if he had done anything or said anything of an offensive nature, he be forgiven. Each of the Council asked likewise. Elder Barlow recounted the purpose of going to Short Creek, over a year ago, to assist the brethren there in accordance with their request, and the clear manifestation of the Spirit which directed the work there. The work that had been accomplished he outlined, and felt that the time had now come for a change in the temporal affairs of the group to be made. He stated the community now consists of about one hundred and fifty souls; they have between twenty and twenty five milk cows, 1 span of mules and two span of horses. Some 1,700 acres of land has been turned in. The crops this year are scant mainly because of lack of water. The canal is now about finished and can be used during the fall and winter in getting a storage of water in the soil.

It was moved by LeGrand and unanimously carried, that inasmuch as the deeds to the respective tracts of land had not been recorded, they be returned to their owners; and that the people of Short Creek be permitted to effect a local organization there. Elder Barlow, being on the ground, may be one of the organization, but is to be released from the active management of the project, devoting his time to the spiritual needs of the Saints there and elsewhere.

With reference to the Magazine TRUTH, the course being followed by the Editor, Elder Musser, was approved and his work commended. It [continued next page]

94 B ☙

was decided to prepare an Open Letter addressed to the President of the United States, his cabinet, Congress, and others pertaining to the salvation of the Constitution of the United States. An outline of the letter was read and approved. The Editor was also authorized to have the Brigham H. Roberts articles on Polygamy, now appearing in TRUTH serially,[2] placed in pamphlet form for more general distribution.
It was thought best that the name of the Editor [should] not appear on the magazine, this being the policy followed to date.

Prayer by John Y. Barlow.
Louis A. Kelsch excused on account of absence from City.

[2] They appeared in *Truth* as follows: 2:17 #2; 2:40 #3; 2:58 #4; 2:78 #5; 2:93 #6; 2:110 #7. These were later followed by articles on plural marriage by leading men and women from the nineteenth century.

95 B ☙

Wednesday, November 25, 1936.
Priesthood held an informal meeting.
Present: Joseph W. Musser, Charles F. Zitting, LeGrand Woolley, and Louis A. Kelsch.

Decided that if Elder Byron Harvey Allred wishes to use the Priesthood article in answer to Brother Widtsoe, in connection with the publishing of the proceedings of his trial for fellowship, there is no objection on the part of the Priesthood.

Elders Musser and Kelsch reported their visit to Short Creek and to Los Angeles, leaving Salt Lake on [the] eighth and returning the morning of the eighteenth.
They were accompanied by Elder Daniel R. Bateman, the only surviving member who can testify as to the proceedings at the meeting held by John Taylor September 27, 1886.[3]
Brother Bateman bore faithful testimonies to the groups at Short Creek and at Los Angeles and Long Beach.

At Short Creek, the brethren reported a lack of union among the Saints caused primarily by the feeling on the part of some that they are being ruled over as a purely Priesthood proposition, and that Brother John Y. Barlow, who is their leader, holds the keys to Priesthood and is the mouthpiece of God to earth. Others took exception to this view, hence the lack of harmony, which trouble was dividing the Saints and rendering the situation very acute for provisions during the coming winter.

---

3 The original manuscript reads "1936." This however is a clear scrivener's error – these minutes were written in 1936 – it is well known that the events in question took place in 1886.

An effort was made to set the Priesthood matter properly before the brethren as follows:
That the Priesthood group holds the Priesthood of Elijah, with special duties given them to keep the spirit and practice of plural marriage alive. That they are not given the duty to colonize groups of Saints. That groups may colonize on their own initiative as they may be led to do, the Priesthood holding itself in readiness to advise and counsel them from time to time on questions germane to the functions and duties of the Priesthood. That the Priesthood group is presided over at present by John Y. Barlow by reason of his seniority in ordination. That any keys possessed are possessed by the group as a body, their powers being expressed through Brother Barlow or such other party as the group may designate. That until the group receives its confirmation, or further instructions, we feel it a duty to confine our activities to the labors appointed to us in our ordination and succeeding instructions. That it should be the policy of the Priesthood to save and not to destroy, and any of the Saints living at Short Creek not wishing to join with the group there in their cooperative plan should be given their liberty to follow their own bent, and not to incur, in consequence, the ill-will of the group.

Notes taken by Joseph W. Musser.

96 B

Minutes of the meeting held Monday, December 14, 1936.
Place: South Temple.
Time: 9:00 a.m.
Joseph presiding and conducting.
Charles opened.
John absent being out of town.

Joseph read a letter to Brice Johnson from a Mr. Roscoe, United Press Agent, inviting him to take an expense paid trip to New York to broadcast over a national system, a statement of his belief.

Unanimously agreed to issue in "Truth" January 1937 an article directed against Joseph Fielding Smith and his misleading statements and articles, particularly concerning plural marriage.[4]

Felt time has come to prepare an obituary for Heber J. Grant, showing the real conditions and circumstances through which Heber has grown to his present status.

Louis closed.

[4] See *Truth* 2:117 #8. Original correspondence between Joseph Fielding Smith and Joseph W. Musser indicates that Joseph Fielding Smith was very unaware that many post-manifesto plural marriages were approved by his father and other members of the twelve apostles of the LDS Church. Although these have been well documented and are well known in today's information age, this information was mostly known by word of mouth during the 1930s and Joseph Fielding Smith was very unwilling to consider any allegations that his father or any other leader of the LDS Church was willing to violate the terms of the 1890 manifesto. Copies of the original letters in the possession of the author.

1937

97 B ☙

Minutes of meeting held Friday, February 26, 1937.
Place: South Temple.
Time: 9:30 a.m.
All present.
John conducting and presiding.
LeGrand opened.
Sacrament administered by Louis and Charles.

Discussed order of passing Sacrament. No one to be given special attention or preference as all partake as equal members. Teachers and Deacons shall not administer the Sacrament. D&C 20:58.

Financial statement for 1936 submitted by Joseph. Statement follows minutes. LeGrand moved and it was voted unanimously to accept same as read.

Joseph asked question – Shall we allow some of the brethren to again continue with a Priesthood class as previously was done? Had been discontinued because of contention. LeGrand moved the meetings be permitted. Unanimous vote.

Joseph spoke on our Apostolic calling, but though we have a senior, no one has been designated by the Lord as the "one man." Our united voice on a question in line with our responsibility and duty is the word of the Lord on the subject. Discussed at considerable length the duties and privileges of our calling.

Joseph closed.

98 B

Report of Receipts and Disbursements of Priesthood Group During the Year 1936, in Salt Lake Division

Balance cash on hand January 1, 1936	$ 80.91
Cash received during the year 1936, as per cash book	$3,057.56
Total cash receipts	**$3,318.47**

Disbursements:

Traveling and Auto. repair expenses	270.22
Miscellaneous books and magazines	26.83
Legal expense (Short Creek cases $200)	211.00
Postage stamps	121.11
Office expense, including rent	93.48
Printing and binding a/c	899.43
Chair rentals for meetings	10.00
Short Creek	738.51
Taxes (Owen's Farm)	10.00
Service Exchange	50.00
Stationery	26.78
Assistance of needy	37.75
Loans returned (Kmetzsch $50; Woolley $50)	100.00
J. W. Musser expense a/o	539.15
Total expenditures	3,134.26
Balance cash on hand	4.21
	3,138.47

99 B

Minutes of the meeting held May 3, 1937.
Place: South Temple.
Time: 12:00 noon.
Joseph, Charles, and Louis present.
Joseph presiding and conducting.
Charles opened.

At Joseph's suggestion, a plan was presented whereby the families of Saints would be visited at least monthly by members of the Priesthood. Similar to ward teaching. Charles was appointed to supervise the work.

Louis closed.

100 B ☙

Minutes of the meeting held October 28, 1937.
Place: South Temple.
Time: 9:00 a.m.
Present: Joseph, LeGrand, and Louis.
Louis opened.
Joseph presided and conducted.

Inasmuch as regular meetings have not been held of late, it was decided to do so every other Wednesday at 9:00 a.m. Same address.

LeGrand read an article on sexual promiscuity in the November 1937, Esquire Magazine. A woman tells her experiences with the opposite sex out of wedlock.

Enjoyed discussing matters of current interest.

LeGrand closed.

101 B ☙

Minutes of meeting held Wednesday, November 3, 1937.
Place: South Temple.
Time: 9:00 a.m.
All present. (John is in Short Creek and automatically excused.)

Joseph presided and conducted.
Charles opened.
Sacrament administered by LeGrand and Louis.

No longer necessary to write minutes in code. Unanimously agreed.

Read from October and November Improvement Era on revelation, spiritual guidance, etc.

Edna Zitting selected to perform anointing for expectant mothers.

Joseph closed.

102 B

Minutes of meeting of November 17, 1937.
Place: South Temple.
Time: 9:00 a.m.
Present: Joseph, LeGrand, and Louis.
Joseph presided and conducted.
LeGrand opened.

LeGrand read a letter from John B. Fine spirit and indicates they are quite favorably prepared for winter. Also an article on Joseph Smith as it will appear in the December issue in "Truth."[1]

Louis dismissed.

103 B

Minutes of meeting held December 15, 1937.

[1] See *Truth* 3:105 #7.

Place: South Temple.
Time: 9:00 a.m.
Joseph, LeGrand, and Louis present.
Joseph presided and conducted.
Louis opened with prayer.

Read from a circular on new moving picture "Polygamy," shown recently at the Million Dollar Theatre in Los Angeles. Very false.

Talked of manner in which business is fettered and straight jacketed by governmental restriction, both state and federal.

LeGrand closed with prayer.

104 B ☙

Special Meeting
December 20, 1937.
Place: South Temple.
Time: 9:00 a.m.
Joseph presided and conducted.
Charles opened with prayer.

Purpose of meeting – To consider a request from Brother Sturm of Chicago, Illinois. To have Joseph come to Chicago for a visit. Brother Sturm will provide the expense money. Joseph related Sherman Lloyd's experience in the Denver branch of the Church, concerning teaching plural marriage. Deemed advisable for Joseph to accept Brother Sturm's invitation.

Louis closed.

Inventory of Book Stock on hand January 1, 1938, exclusive of Truth Magazines and books gotten out by Priesthood

3 copies miscellaneous pamphlets bound	3.00	Sale Value	9.00
8 copies miscellaneous pamphlets bound	2.50	Sale Value	20.00
8 copies Truth Vol. 1 & 2 pamphlets bound	5.00	Sale Value	30.00
8 copies Truth Vol. 2 pamphlets bound	3.00	Sale Value	24.00
1 copies Inspired Bible		Sale Value	3.50
3 copies Inspired Bible	1.50	Sale Value	4.50
3 copies Book of Mormon	.50	Sale Value	1.50
2 copies Doctrine and Covenants	1.00	Sale Value	2.00
2 copies Pearl of Great Price	.50	Sale Value	1.00
8 copies Inspired translation compared	.25	Sale Value	2.00
6 copies Lectures on Faith	.15	Sale Value	.90
1 copies Family Bible (old)		Sale Value	2.00
250 copies Plural Marriage by Roberts	.30	Sale Value	75.00
			175.40

Less paid in Roberts Books not included in "Store Stock"	$60.00
	$145.40

1938

105 B

January 12, 1938. (Wednesday)
Place: South Temple.
Time: 9:00 a.m.
All present.
John presiding and conducting.
LeGrand opened.
Sacrament administered by Joseph and Charles.

John said the time has come to cleanse ourselves and forget past feelings and misunderstandings toward each other. Must maintain and keep alive the truth but not our job to set God's House in order.[1]

Each brother expressed his feelings concerning our calling. Each asked forgiveness of the others for any offense. All grievances forgiven and forgotten.

Discussed other matters of interest relative to giving blessings. Must be more careful, cautious, and wise.

LeGrand led in the prayer circle.
Charles closed with prayer.

106 B

February 2, 1938.
Place: South Temple.
Time: 9:00 a.m.
? opened with prayer.
Joseph presided and conducted.

---

[1] Lorin C. Woolley taught that "the Church, the kingdom of God, and the Council of Friends ... constitute the House of God." *Reminiscences* 1:10 (A Discussion with Olive Woolley Coombs)(6/–/1971).

Present: Joseph, Charles, LeGrand, & Louis; John in Short Creek.

Joseph presented the financial report for year 1937.

Moved and unanimously accepted as read. Statement follows these minutes.

Brother E. P. Williams has asked Joseph to come to California. California Saints usually send transportation expenses for such trips.
Agreeable with all that he go.

Read and approved the concluding article of "It Is Written" as published in Truth.[2]

The young people of our group are desirous of organizing a gospel study class and ask our approval of same.
Unanimously approved.

Discussed the United Order. Brother George Woodruff has expressed a desire to consecrate his home, though it has an indebtedness of about $600.

Charles dismissed.

Report of Receipts and Disbursements of Priesthood Group, Salt Lake City, During the Year 1937

Balance cash on hand January 1, 1937	$ 4.21
Cash received during the year 1937, as per cash book	$3,072.68
Total Cash	$3,076.89

Disbursements:

Rent (Includes Office, P.O. Box, Chairs, etc.)	143.25
Office fixtures and supplies	*102.76

2 See *Truth* 3:93 #6.

Library (Books and Magazines)	**67.79
Stock (Includes books for sale and binding)	§202.54
Postage	118.68
Transportation	§§148.53
Printing (Truth, Robert's Marriage, etc.)	1,001.29
Special Assistance	102.50
Office help	7.75
Bank charges	3.42
Miscellaneous	#91.90
J. W. Musser, Maintenance a/c	910.00
Total Disbursements	2,900.41
Balance Cash on hand Jan. 1, 1938	176.48
	3,076.89

* Includes $51.94 for materials used in reforming office. Work contributed by Brethren.

** Includes $34.40 in books purchased and contributed by Heber K. Cleveland.

§ Receipts from book sales for year	221.56
Books on hand and paid for	115.40
	336.96

§§ Includes two trips to California and one trip to Chicago, the major part of the expense in each case being contributed for the purpose, and shown in cash receipts

This item includes $41.90 paid for chairs for Priesthood needs; and $50.00 received from sale of Wheat contributed by C.O. Holm, and used in Granary construction.

107 B

March 2, 1938.
Place: South Temple.
Time: 9:00 a.m.
Present: Joseph, LeGrand, & Louis.
Joseph presided and conducted.
Louis opened with prayer.

LeGrand read an article on the Church Security Program by Martha Emery in the February 12, 1938 issue of the magazine "The Nation." Reveals a sad situation.

Considered the proposition of Brother Farnsworth to start a cooperative movement.

Discussed the possibilities of attempting a humble beginning of the United Order. Several of the brethren have offered their possessions for that cause. Alright to accomplish all that can be [accomplished], but not place the responsibility on the council, as a body.

LeGrand closed.

108 B ☙

March 16, 1938.
Place: South Temple.
Time: 9:00 a.m.
Joseph, Charles, LeGrand, & Louis present.
Joseph presided and conducted.

Read and discussed correspondence between Joseph and E. P. Williams of Los Angeles. Date of March 10 & 12, 1938. Question asked by Brother Williams – From whom of the Priesthood are we to take direction when there is a confliction in instruction? and, Is it possible the Priesthood is out of order as is the Church?
We must give no instruction as a Priesthood without first counseling together and being united.

Charles read from the "Quorum Bulletin for the quorums of the Melchizedek Priesthood and Gospel Doctrine" of the LDS Church, for First Quarter 1938. Lesson 10, entitled "The Nephite's Sin."
LeGrand read an answering article entitled, "The Book of Mormon & Polygamy," prepared by Joseph to be published in Truth.[3]

---

3 This was published in the April, 1938 number of *Truth* 3:177 #11.

With some suggested changes, article approved.

LeGrand closed.

109 B ᘓ

March 30, 1938.
Place: South Temple.
Time: 9:00 a.m.
Joseph presided and conducted.
LeGrand opened.

Joseph read a letter from John wherein he says the recently published "Adam-God" pamphlet is the finest thing out so far. He plans on coming up for conference. Poverty is increasing. Freezing weather in St. George.

H. Ensign, of Kansas City, asks what his rights are in contemplation of a trial for teaching false doctrine. He has been teaching the Gospel from "Truth," in opposition to present church rule.

Discussed world events and personalities.

Louis closed.

110 B ᘓ

April 6, 1938, Savior's Birthday.
Place: South Temple.
Time: 9:00 a.m.
All present, John being home from Short Creek.
John presided & conducted by LeGrand.
John opened with prayer.
Sacrament Administered by Joseph & Louis.

John said he could see an improvement in the spirit of things since his last visit with us. Also, that the Adam-God booklet, just published, was the finest on that subject in this dispensation.

Don't get too hard on President Grant and the leaders; they are doing their work well.

One hundred sixty-two present at the meeting last Sunday night at Carl Jentzsch's.

People have not gone hungry this year in Short Creek.

Price and Elmer Johnson have pulled out with their land and the saw mill. They are not with the Short Creek group.

Joseph said he could see a bolder attitude on the part of the people to read and learn the truth for themselves.

Paid subscriptions to Truth have increased materially. Sending out, monthly, about seven hundred copies.

Question by Joseph: What should be our policy regarding gathering?
Must wait more specific instructions from the Lord before counseling gathering, though encourage Saints to be lead by the spirit of the Lord.

The spirit prevailing in our meetings, generally, among the Saints, is not confined to plural marriage alone but the fullness of the Gospel.

All present expressed their feelings spiritually and temporally. Must be patient, waiting on the Lord for direction regarding United Order, Gathering, etc.

Charles to help Brother Worth Kilgrow get someone to share with him in farming a forty-acre tract of land on West 21 South Salt Lake City.

Decided unanimously to print "The Coming Crisis" and "It Is Written," in pamphlet form, as soon as possible.

Charles Closed.

111 B

April 12, 1938.
Place: South Temple.
Time: 9:00 a.m.
Joseph, LeGrand, & Louis present.
Joseph presided & conducted.
Louis opened.

Council deemed it timely for Tuesday night class to study United Order. The class is very desirous to do so.

Photostatic copy of Revelation of 1886 to be reproduced in Truth.[4]

LeGrand read an article, "Comments on Conference Topics," prepared for Truth. First time Truth has treated at length Church [...][5]

112 B

May 11, 1938.
Place: South Temple.

[4] For some reason, this was not published until the following October. See *Truth* 4:84-85 #5. The copy is a negative of the original. Easier to read copies have been reproduced since this original publication.
[5] The editor's copy of the original manuscript becomes illegible at this point.

Time: 9:00 a.m.
Joseph, Charles, LeGrand, & Louis present.
? presided & conducted.
Charles opened.

Considered articles on United Order,[6] Declaration of Faith,[7] and Discourse by Brigham Young,[8] prepared for June Truth.

LeGrand closed.

113 B

May 25, 1938.
Place: South Temple.
Time: 9:00 a.m.
Joseph, Charles, LeGrand, & Louis present.
Joseph presided & conducted.
Charles Opened.

Joseph presented a letter and an article entitled "Thank You Short Creek" from Reed Lauritzen, which he desires to print in Truth.

Agreed to prepare a brief, qualifying, editorial and if John sanctions it, to print the article for what it is worth as presenting the view of the opposition.

LeGrand read two articles prepared for Truth, one entitled "The Events of July,"[9] and one by Eliza R. Snow, "The Loathsome Ulcer-What Is It?"[10] Also two poems by Eliza R. Snow, "Ode for the Fourth Day of July" and "To Elder John Taylor."[11]

---

6 See *Truth* 4:9 #1.
7 See *Truth* 4:5 #1.
8 See *Truth* 4:1 #1.
9 See *Truth* 4:21 #2.
10 See *Truth* 4:27 #2.
11 See *Truth* 4:38 #2 (it was actually entitled *Fourth of July Ode*) and 4:3 #2.

Louis dismissed.

114 B ☙

June 8, 1938.
Place: South Temple.
Time: 9:00 a.m.
Joseph, Charles, & Louis present.
Joseph presided and Louis conducted.
Charles opened with prayer.

Joseph read a letter from John Y. Barlow, regarding Reed Lauritzen's little treatise on Short Creek, together with a proposed editorial. John says suit ourselves, but he will have nothing to do with Reed's article.
Voted not to publish it.

Joseph read a follow-up article on United Order,[12] prepared for July Truth, and also an article "The Divine Prescription," written in 1932, and now deemed wise to publish in Truth.

Joseph closed.

115 B ☙

December 19, 1938.
Place: South Temple.
Time: 9:00 a.m.
Present: Joseph, Charles, LeGrand, & Louis.
Joseph presided & conducted.
LeGrand opened.
Sacrament Administered by Charles & Louis.

---

12 See *Truth* 4:32 #2.

LeGrand – There is no man on earth holding the Apostleship, is there? Joseph – None that we know of that is fully qualified.

Discussed Short Creek and how it has failed, apparently. The brethren also having lost all they had in Big Bend.

Each expressed his love and esteem for the other members of the council. No ill feelings against each other.

A letter from E. F. Barlow, Short Creek, indicates the brethren there have organized themselves independent of John Barlow and will carry on accordingly.
Meets our approval.

Discussed current events.

Joseph dismissed.

1939

116 B ☙

January 2, 1939.
Place: South Temple.
Time: 9:00 a.m.
Joseph, Charles, LeGrand, & Louis present.
Joseph presided & conducted.
Louis opened with prayer.
Sacrament Administered by Joseph & Charles.

Read a letter Joseph had written to John. Sweet spirited and sincerely concerned for John and his efforts there. (Near Cedar City).

A letter from E. F. Barlow was read, showing the brethren in Short Creek still hold us responsible for their economic troubles there.
We, living in this part of the county disclaimed our responsibility to Short Creek in September 1936 after a visit there, at which time they refused to accept our resolution concerning them.

Several of the brethren were selected to attend a special meeting the first Sunday of each month. Purpose, to have a special prayer circle and also to organize or appoint the brethren to go in pairs and visit a given number of the group families each month.

Charles closed.

117 B ☙

January 30, 1939.
Place: South Temple.
Time: 9:00 a.m.
Present: Joseph, Charles, LeGrand, & Louis.

Joseph presided & conducted.
Sacrament administered by Charles & Louis.

Brother Denos desires to organize a singing chorus among our people, to which our council has no objections.

Read the financial statement for 1938.
Moved and unanimously voted that we accept same as read.
Statement follows minutes of this meeting.

Read, over the signature of Andrew Jensen, that thirty-six percent of the marriage among LDS are performed in the Temples.

Read an article on healthful eating by Rulon Allred. Good for publication. Deals especially with milk, meat, diet, etc.

Also, an item prepared for Truth showing that plural marriage was performed and acknowledged as late as 1899 in the case of William Daines, a Patriarch living in Preston, Idaho.[1]

Read a letter from Price W. Johnson, being a copy of one he sent to several of the leading authorities of the Church. Deals with their treatment of him in persecuting and prosecuting for his belief in and living of plural marriage.

LeGrand closed, being mouth for circle prayer.

<u>Receipts and Disbursements of Priesthood Group, during the year 1938</u>

Balance cash on hand January 1, 1938	$ 176.48
Cash received during the year 1938	<u>$3,993.19</u>
Total	$4,169.67

<u>Disbursements:</u>

1 See *Truth* 4:195 #10.

Rent (Includes office, Post Office, Chairs, etc.)	217.25
Office fixtures & supplies, telephone, etc.	52.99
Library	59.50
Store stock	290.37
Postage	140.97
Transportation: trains, gas & oil	210.38
Printing	1,040.89
Special Assistance	178.85
Office help	64.40
Bank charges	11.01
Editorial expense	1,500.00
Miscellaneous	149.42
Total expenditures	3,916.03
Balance cash on hand	253.64
	4,169.67

Of the above receipts, approximately $185.00 came from sale of books and literature. There is approximately $300.00 of value in Stock.

118 B

Minutes of the meeting held May 16, 1939.
Place: 744 East South Temple.
Time: 9:00 a.m.
Present: Joseph, Charles, LeGrand, and Louis; John being in Cedar.
Joseph presided and LeGrand conducted.
Charles opened with prayer.
Sacrament administered by Louis and Joseph.

Agree to increase size of type used in printing "Truth."
Plans to publish a ready reference of the Doctrine of Marriage[2] were presented and passed unanimously.
LeGrand read the preface, also an article "Doctrinal Lectures," to be published in "Truth," as also an anniversary editorial[3] beginning the fifth volume.
Plan to devote a page of each issue of "Truth" to questions and answers passed.

---

2 See *Truth* 5:1 #1.
3 See *Truth* 5:11 #1.

Joseph closed.

119 B

July 31, 1939.
Place: 744 East South Temple St.
Time: 9:00 a.m.
Present: Joseph, LeGrand, and Louis.
Joseph presided and Louis conducted.
LeGrand opened.
Sacrament administered by Joseph and Louis.

Joseph read a letter from Brother Lawson of San Diego, California Asking several questions which were discussed and proper answers prepared.

Brother Melvin J. Ballard died about 8:00 p.m. last night in the L.D.S. hospital.

Considered item for Truth, "That Manifesto Imbroglio."[4] With some additional comments, approved.

Joseph closed.

120 B

August 7, 1939.
Place: 744 East South Temple St.
Time: 9:00 a.m.
Present: John, Joseph, Charles, LeGrand, and Louis; John being in from Cedar.
John presided and Joseph conducted.
Louis opened.

---

4 See *Truth* 5:85 #4.

LeGrand read an article on the death of Melvin J. Ballard, as prepared for Truth, also the following items, "That Double Life Enigma," "Ignorance," and "Questionnaire Box."[5]

Question by Brother Wroth Kilgrow – I am losing my farm, should I join Kingston's in Bountiful? They offer me temporal security.
We, as council, cannot advise such a move.

Sacrament administered by Charles and LeGrand.
John, as mouth for the prayer circled, closed.

121 B ☙

August 14, 1939.
Place: 744 East South Temple.
Time: 9:00 a.m.
John presided and conducted.
Present: John, Joseph, Charles, LeGrand, and Louis.
Joseph opened.
Sacrament Administered by Charles and Louis.

LeGrand suggested we approach certain good men with the view in mind of encouraging them to prepare themselves that the Lord may work with them.
Moved that Joseph and LeGrand be appointed to carry out the suggestion.

Discussed matters of current interest and importance.

LeGrand closed, being mouth for the prayer circle.

122 B ☙

[5] See *Truth* 5:116 #5.

September 4, 1939.
Place: 744 East South Temple.
Present: John, Joseph, Louis, and Roy Johnson. Charles out of town and LeGrand excused.
John presided and conducted.
Louis opened with prayer.

Have met to consider a defense for Richard Jessop and Fred Jessop of New Harmony, Utah, who have been arrested on charges of cohabitation. Their wives also being subpoenaed. Trial is set for September 19, 1939 at St. George, Utah. They were arrested September 1, 1939, the day hostilities commenced in Europe between Germany and Poland.
Joseph has prepared an appeal, to be sent to our friends and sympathizers in all parts of the country, soliciting their support financially and morally in fighting the case.
Decided to interview Claude Barnes as a prospective attorney for the case; to meet him tomorrow at 10:00 a.m. in his office.

Joseph closed with prayer.

123 B

September 11, 1939.
Place: 744 East South Temple.
Time: 9:00 a.m.
Present: John, Joseph, Charles, LeGrand, and Louis.
John presided and conducted.
Charles opened.

Considered case of Richard and Fred Jessop.
LeGrand moved we employ an attorney to fight the case through the law courts of the state.
Unanimously approved.
LeGrand moved we employ attorney Claude Barnes at the best monetary figure obtainable.

Considered item for Truth, "Was There a Revelation?"[6]

Louis, as mouth for the prayer circle, closed.

124 B

September 25, 1939.
Place: 744 East South Temple.
Time: 9:00 a.m.
Present: John, Joseph, LeGrand, and Louis.
John presided and Louis conducted.
Joseph opened.
Sacrament administered by John and LeGrand.

Discussed the trial at St. George.

Read an appeal for financial assistance to be known as the defense fund. Receipts to be used in fighting the unconstitutional laws framed against celestial marriage. "An Explanation,"[7] prepared for Truth, was read. Deals with Francis M. Darter's latest leaflet on "The Son of Perdition."

Read the "White Horse" prophecy by Joseph Smith. Not considered authentic enough to republish without more detailed information.[8]

John, as mouth for the prayer circle, closed, after presenting to the Lord the names of those who were leaders of the opposition in the recent trial.

---

6 See *Truth* 5:107 #5.
7 See *Truth* 5:119 #5.
8 See *Minutes* 10a fn 52. Burgess' testimony on this issue was likely not available to the council at this time.

125 B

October 2, 1939.
Place: 744 East South Temple.
Time: 9:00 a.m.
Present: John, Joseph, Charles, LeGrand, and Louis.
John presided and conducted.
Charles opened.

Brother Francis M. Darter asks our opinion on his publishing more pamphlets, "Son of Perdition." He has distributed nearly five thousand copies so far.
Move we take same stand as before and if he goes ahead, he does so on his own responsibility.
Unanimously approved.

Read a correspondence between J. L. Athay and David O. McKay.

Considered item for Truth, "A Vital Omission."

Sacrament administered by Charles and LeGrand.
Joseph, mouth for the prayer circle.

126 B

October 9, 1939.
Place: 744 East South Temple.
Time: 9:00 a.m.
Present: John, Joseph, LeGrand, and Louis.
John presided and conducted.
LeGrand opened.

Considered items for Truth – "Honor and Obey,"[9] "Liberty and Freedom"[10] and "John Taylor."[11]

As mouth for the prayer circle, Joseph closed.

127 B

October 30, 1939.
Place: 744 East South Temple.
Time: 9:00 a.m.
Present: John, Joseph, LeGrand, and Louis.
John presided and Joseph conducted.
John opened.

Considered item for Truth, "Record Purging."[12]

Read letter from LeRoy A. Wilson concerning Francis M. Darter. Also instructions to Masons of 32, 31, 30 degree declaring Satan the true God of this world.

Discussed current topics.

Louis closed, being mouth for the prayer circle.

128 B

November 27, 1939.
Place: 744 East South Temple.
Time: 9:00 a.m.
Present: John, Joseph, Charles, LeGrand, and Louis.
John presided and Louis conducted.
Louis opened.

---

9 See *Truth* 5:121 #6.
10 See *Truth* 5:130 #6.
11 See *Truth* 5:131 #6.
12 See *Truth* 5:155 #7.

Considered items for Truth.

Moved that Lyman Jessop be appointed superintendent of the Sunday School with Ed Christensen and A. Pettit as assistants and that Arnold Boss and Axel Fors be appointed as teachers of the adult class.
Unanimously approved.

Reorganized leadership of the lady's Tuesday night class. Moved that Sister E. Morrison be appointed leader with Sister Ann Boss and Leah Dockstader as assistants.
Unanimously approved.

Sacrament administered by LeGrand and John.
Charles, as mouth for the prayer circle, closed.

129 B

December 4, 1939.
Place: 744 East South Temple.
Time: 9:00 a.m.
Present: Joseph, Charles, LeGrand, and Louis; John being in Cedar.
Joseph presided and conducted.
Charles opened.

Considered item for Truth, "A Priesthood Issue."[13]

Joseph closed with prayer.

130 B

December 11, 1939.

---

13 See *Truth* 5:179 #8.

Place: 744 East South Temple.
Time: 9:00 a.m.
Present: John, Joseph, Charles, LeGrand, and Louis.
John presided and LeGrand conducted.
John opened.
Sacrament administered by Joseph and Louis.

Decided to meet once a month (the first Monday) rather than weekly. Special meetings may be held if necessary.

John told of his experience in hearing a voice which counseled him in things pertaining to our present condition. Occurred at Cedar. Saints to get a hedge of the Lord's spirit around them as protection. Heavens soon to speak. Others gone on are praying for the Lord to hasten the setting in order of His house. When we stop plural marriage, we cease living Celestial Marriage.

Discussed current events.

All elders have been called home from European nations.

John was mouth for the prayer circle.

1940

131 B ☙

January 21, 1940.
Place: 809 East 7 South.
Time: 10:00 a.m.
Present: John, Joseph, Charles, LeGrand, and Louis.
John presided and Joseph conducted.
LeGrand opened.
Sacrament administered by Charles and John.

Louis performed the ordinance of feet washing for Charles, he having been absent for that ordinance at a similar meeting a month previous.

Joseph gave a report of his recent trip to California. Have had exceptionally heavy rains there this winter. Read an outline of the sermons he delivered while there.

Read correspondence between Joseph W. Musser and Israel A. Smith of the Reorganized Church.

Read the annual financial report, including the defense fund. Moved and unanimously approved to accept report as read. Copy follows these minutes.

Read letters of Joseph T. Jones, Rexburg, Idaho. He sent two to his Stake Presidency and one to Rudger Clawson.

Charles was mouth for the prayer circle.

132 B ☙

February 5, 1940.
Place: 744 East South Temple.
Time: 9:00 a.m.
Present: John, Joseph, Charles, LeGrand, and Louis.

John presided and conducted.
LeGrand opened.
Sacrament administered by Joseph and Charles.

Discussed the United Order and were agreed that in order to establish it, revelation and direction from heaven will be necessary.

Considered items for Truth – "Questions On Priesthood,"[1] "Record Purging,"[2] and "Ready References."[3]

Louis closed, being mouth for the prayer circle.

Receipts and Disbursements of Priesthood Group
Year 1939

Balance cash on hand January 1, 1939		$ 253.64
Cash received during the year 1939 - General		$3,942.01
- Defense		$ 677.65
Total cash receipts		$4,873.30
Disbursements		
On General Account:		
Rent (Office, chairs, P.O. Box)		252.55
Office (Furniture, stationery, telephone, etc.)		82.28
Postage		156.10
Printing		1,057.34
Transportation		192.38
Library		58.60
Stock		126.92
Special help in office		56.25
Special help in group		108.75
Missionary help		96.00
Chairs, - payment on purchase of		10.00
Editorial expense		1,800.00
	Total expenditures	3,997.17
On Defense Account:		
Attorney's fees	450.00	

[1] See *Truth* 5:217 #10.
[2] See *Truth* 5:225 #10.
[3] See *Truth* 5:231 #10.

Postage	11.00		
Printing circular letter	4.59		
Printing Abstract	17.34		
Printing Brief	18.36		
Court Steno. For Abstract	17.50		
Expense attending trial	50.00		
Misc. travel expense & other help for defs	74.65	643.44	4,640.61
Balance cash - General fund	198.48		
- Defense fund	34.21		232.69
Sales from stock, approximately	112.00		
Paid subscribers for TRUTH	338.00		
Monthly distribution of TRUTH approx.	850.00		
Comparisons: Cash receipts for 1937			3,072.68
Cash receipts for 1938			3,993.19
Cash receipts for 1939			4,619.66

133 B

March 4, 1940.
Place: 744 East South Temple.
Time: 9:00 a.m.
Present: John, Joseph, Charles, LeGrand, and Louis.
John presided and conducted.
Joseph opened with prayer.
Sacrament administered by LeGrand and Louis.

Moved Charles and Louis investigate, with authority to purchase, ten dozen folding chairs.
Unanimously approved

Moved that one thousand copies of "A Priesthood Issue," as published in January, February, and March 1940 Truth, be published in pamphlet form.

Considered items for April, 1940 Truth.

Joseph, as mouth. for the prayer circle, closed.

134 B

April 1, 1940.
Place: 744 East South Temple.
Time: 9:00 a.m.
Present: John, Joseph, Charles, LeGrand, and Louis.
John presided and Joseph conducted.
John opened.
Sacrament administered by Charles and Louis.

Charles authorized to confer the Melchizedek Priesthood upon Blaine Thompson (Kilgrow) (16) and ordain him an elder.
Considered case of Edward Granger and Clela Stokes. Clela desires to be released. Edward is in Florida.
Moved she wait awhile and not to live with him if he returns.

Joseph read a letter from Price Johnson, Short Creek, desiring direction concerning their meetings, who shall preside, etc?
Decided to postpone action until after April conference.

Considered item for Truth – "Some McConkie Errors."[4]

LeGrand, as mouth for the prayer circle, closed.

135 B

May 6, 1940.
Place: 744 East South Temple.
Time: 9:00 a.m.
Present: John, Joseph, LeGrand, and Louis.
John presided and LeGrand conducted.
Sacrament administered by Joseph and Louis.

---

[4] See *Truth* 5:278 #12.

John said that John Woolley told him the One Mighty and Strong was Joseph Smith and said "I know it my boy because I know it."[5]

Considered items for Truth.

John, as mouth for the prayer circle, closed.

136 B ☙

July 1, 1940.
Place: 744 East South Temple.
Time: 9:00 a.m.
Present: John, Joseph, LeGrand, and Louis.
John presided and conducted.
John opened.
Sacrament administered by Joseph and Louis.

Considered items for Truth – "Mathias F. Cowley,"[6] "Voting Rights of Saints,"[7] "Burning Prophecies," and "The Proof of a Prophet."[8]

LeGrand, as mouth for the prayer circle, closed.

---

[5] Apostle Moses Thatcher first taught that the one mighty and strong referred to in the D&C was Joseph Smith. George Q. Cannon opposed Thatcher's prophecies and teachings on this matter but these ideas circulated so thoroughly among the saints that it was eventually discussed in the United States Congress – during the Reed Smoot hearings. See Horne, Dennis B., Ed, *An Apostle's Record: The Journals of Abraham H. Cannon*, Gnolaum Books, 2004. See entries for the following dates: 8/20/1886; 10/7/1889; & 2/1/1890; See also 59th Congress, 1st Session, Document #486, *Proceedings Before the Committee on Privileges and Election of the United States Senate: In the Matter of the Protest Against the Right of Hon. Reed Smoot, a Senator from the State of Utah, to Hold His Seat*, Washington: (Government Printing Office: 1906) , 1:278-80; and *MS* 15:205.

[6] See *Truth* 6:63 #3.

[7] See *Truth* 6:59 #3.

[8] See *Truth* 6:81 #4.

137 B

August 13, 1940.
Place: 744 East South Temple.
Time: 9:00 a.m.
Present: John, Joseph, Charles, LeGrand, and Louis.
John Presided and conducted.
Sacrament administered by Joseph and Charles.
Joseph opened.

Considered items for Truth – "Steps To Apostacy,"[9] "Police – Not Spies,"[10] and "Ready Reference On Celestial Marriage – Legal Aspect of Polygamy."[11]

Question – Is it permissible to hold group dances each Friday night before the regular Sunday meetings, which are held the second and fourth Sunday of each month?
Yes.

Read minutes of meeting of August 4, 1940 held at 27 South and Highland Drive, pertaining to Brother Francis M. Darter.
Discussed at considerable length the conditions surrounding the case.
Postponed definite action until a later date.

LeGrand was mouth for the prayer circle.

Charles closed with prayer.

138 B

September 9, 1940.
Place: 744 East South Temple.

---

[9] See *Truth* 6:83 #4. The spelling error was retained in the publication.
[10] See *Truth* 6:89 #3.
[11] See *Truth* 6:90 #3.

Time: 9:00 a.m.
Present: John, Joseph, and Louis.
John presided and conducted.
Louis opened.

Considered items for October Truth – "Brigham Young,"[12] "Evidence and Reconciliations."[13]

Read letter of Brother Otto H. Olschewski of Brooklyn, New York Also his notice of disfellowshipment from the church by the New York Stake Presidency.
Joseph to answer Brother Otto's letter.

Joseph, as mouth for the prayer circle, closed.

139 B ☙

October 7, 1940.
Place: 744 East South Temple.
Time: 9:00 a.m.
Present: John, Joseph, Charles, and Louis; LeGrand excused.
John presided and Joseph conducted.
Charles opened.
Sacrament administered by Louis and John.

Read correspondence with Saints in New York. They want one of our brethren to come visit them and seem to be willing to finance the trip.
Joseph to make further inquiry.

Brother Francis M. Darter asks – Can we sanction a second edition of his leaflet, "End of Our Generation of Christ's Section Coming?"
Unanimously voted no. Neither did we pass on his first edition.

---

[12] See *Truth* 6:111 #5.
[13] See *Truth* 6:107 #5.

John, as mouth for the prayer circle, closed.

140 B

November 25, 1940.
Place: 744 East South Temple.
Time: 9:00 a.m.
Present: John, Joseph, Charles, LeGrand, and Louis.
John presided and conducted.
Louis opened.
Sacrament administered by LeGrand and Charles.

Read a letter from Brother M. Bautista of Old Mexico under date of October 21, 1940.

Read a letter from Roy Wilson, dated October 23, 140 at Veyo, Utah. Asks our financial aid in preparing weapons of war.
Concluded we are not prepared financially or morally to support his offer.

Recounted some of the experiences and impressions of our recent trip to the eastern states. (John, Joseph, Charles, and Louis.)

Joseph, as mouth for the prayer circle, closed.

141 B

Special Meeting.
December 19, 1940.
Place: 744 East South Temple.
Time: 9:00 a.m.
Present: John, Joseph, Charles, LeGrand, and Louis.
John presided and Joseph conducted.

Charles opened.

Purpose of meeting – To consider the advisability of recommending a "death benefit" insurance policy to the group.
Decided to await more favorable developments concerning the present board of directors of the company. The company is organized agreeable to the Utah State laws governing insurance companies.

Considered letter from the New York brethren in which they inquire as to gathering to the Rocky Mountains.
Decided to encourage them to make the move.

Joseph received and read a very bitter letter from Edward Granger.[14] Edward is in Tampa Florida with his mother, being permitted to go there from the Utah State Mental Hospital on the condition he will never return to the State of Utah.
Joseph also read his answer to Edward.

Louis closed with prayer.

[14] cf. *Minutes* 134b.

1941

142 B

January 6, 1941.
Place: 744 East South Temple.
Time: 9:00 a.m.
Present: John, Joseph, Charles, LeGrand, and Louis.
John presided and Charles conducted.
Joseph opened.
Sacrament administered by Louis and LeGrand.

Read letters from some of the New York brethren showing a splendid spirit. (Brothers A. Austendorf, A. Olschewski and Hans Doelling)
Read Joseph's answer, under direction, to the New York brethren regarding gathering to the Rocky Mountains. Encouraged them to gather.

Beginning January 1, 1941, all applicants for Temple recommends have to sign a questionnaire as printed on the back of the recommend. Contains seven questions.

We have a copy of "Progress of the Church" for December 19, 1940, which contains a printed list of the names of many who have been handled for their sympathy towards plural marriage. The leaflet is issued monthly by [… .][1]

143 B

February 5, 1941.
Place: 744 East South Temple.
Time: 9:00 a.m.
Present: John, Joseph, Charles, LeGrand, and Louis.
John presided and LeGrand conducted.

1 The remaining portion of these minutes is missing in the editor's copy of the manuscript.

John opened with prayer.
Sacrament administered by Joseph and Louis.

A letter was read from Brother Bautista who lives in Mexico, saying he was operating there under his own authority. He asks us to help sell some of his books at $1.00 a copy.

Mr. Berry, a Navaho Indian, has asked for baptism for himself and wife. Deemed wise to have Charles contact him, in connection with Brothers Thomas and Jimison, to determine the worthiness of his request.

Read article for Truth, "A Defense of Truth."

Discussed storing of foodstuffs. Also, needs for a larger gathering place. To consider further.

Louis, as mouth for the prayer circle, closed the meeting.

144 B ☙

March 10, 1941.
Place: 744 East South Temple.
Time: 9:00 a.m.
Present: John, Joseph, Charles, LeGrand, and Louis.
John presided and conducted.
Louis opened with prayer.
Dispensed with the Sacrament.

Read financial report for year 1940, a copy of which follows these minutes.
Moved and voted unanimously to approve report as read.

Read letter from Brother Fritz Kempe of New York regarding tithing.

Considered items for Truth, "Does This Mean Reform,"[2] "A Timely Caution"[3] and "Church Jurisprudence."[4]

Charles closed with prayer.

145 B

April 14, 1941.
Place: 744 East South Temple.
Time: 9:00 a.m.
Present: John, Joseph, Charles, LeGrand, and Louis.
John presided and LeGrand conducted.
John opened with prayer.
Sacrament administered by Joseph and Louis.

Considered items for Truth dealing with the life of Apostle John W. Taylor,[5] also "The Apologist Persists"[6] and "A Reformed Policy."[7]

Moved we buy one hundred metal, folding chairs for use in our meetings. Charles to have charge of the purchase. Unanimously approved.

Read letter from Brother Ayres of Toronto, Canada. Displays a beautiful spirit.

Charles, as mouth for the prayer circle, closed.

<u>Receipts and Disbursements of Priesthood Council</u>
<u>Year 1940</u>

---

[2] See *Truth* 6:251 #11.
[3] See *Truth* 6:254 #11.
[4] See *Truth* 6:257 #11.
[5] See *Truth* 6:265 #12.
[6] See *Truth* 6:279 #12.
[7] See *Truth* 6:281 #12.

Balance cash on hand January 1, 1940	$ 198.48
Cash received during year 1940	$5,209.36
Total cash	$5,407.84

Disbursements	
Rent: Office, chairs, P.O. Box, garage	242.85
Postage	145.52
Office (Furniture, stationery, phone, etc.)	106.44
Office help	177.75
Printing and supplies a/c Magazine	1,069.44
Transportation	524.84
(Railroad, bus, Automobile, including Auto. Repairs)	
Library (Books, pamphlets, periodicals, etc.)	45.05
Stock for sale	218.74
Special Assistance	524.28
Editorial Exp.	1,800.00
Miscellaneous (Legal, typewriter, coal for office, chairs, etc.)	345.21
Total Disbursements	5,200.12
Balance cash on hand	207.72

Comparisons		
Cash receipts	1937	3,072.68
	1938	3,993.19
	1939	4,615.66
	1940	5,209.36

Disbursements in excess of those of 1939 on same items:	
Transportation	332.46
Special help	415.53
Miscellaneous	345.21
Stock for sale	91.82
	1,185.02

Stock sales	1939	approximately	112.00
Stock sales	1940	approximately	200.00

146 B

Special Meeting.
Monday, April 21, 1941.
Place: 744 East South Temple
Time: 9:00 a.m.
Present: John, Joseph, Charles, LeGrand, and Louis.
Louis opened with prayer.

John arose and said the other night, he had two names presented to him by the spirit, who should be called to fill up this quorum, Brother LeRoy Johnson of Cedar City, Utah and Marion Hammon of Salt Lake City, Utah.
LeGrand said he felt the call should be confirmed by a personal visit from the other side, as, according to our understanding, has been the case in previous callings.
Joseph suggested we fast Saturday and meet here at 9:00 a.m. Sunday. In the meantime, see if a definite answer can be obtained concerning this matter, also that a sexual fast be observed. Unanimously agreed.

Charles dismissed.

147 B ☙

Special Meeting.
Sunday, April 27, 1941.
Place: 744 East South Temple.
Time: 9:00 a.m.
Present: John, Joseph, Charles, LeGrand, and Louis.
John presided and conducted.
Charles opened with prayer.

This meeting concludes a week of prayerful consideration upon the names of LeRoy Johnson and Marion Hammon, whose names, John said, were presented to him by the spirit to be called to fill this quorum.
John said, "I am convinced enough of the truthfulness of these callings to take the responsibility as the senior member of the council.
None of us has received a direct answer to his prayers but feel in no position to dictate or try to direct those senior to us.
Joseph moved, that recognizing John as the senior member of our quorum, we accept his recommendation as coming from

the Lord, endorse the men named, and await further direction from the other side.
Unanimously agreed.

Decided to meet each Monday morning at 9:00 a.m. for a study class. LeGrand to take the lead.

Joseph closed with prayer.

148 B ☙

Monday, May 19, 1941.
Place: 744 East South Temple.
Time: 9:00 a.m.
Present: John, Joseph, Charles, Marion Hammon, and Louis.
John presided and Joseph conducted.

John said he had had assurance and set LeRoy Johnson of Cedar apart and since coming home, Joseph, at John's request, had set Marion Hammon apart as members of this council.
Joseph read Roy Johnson's patriarchal blessing given in 1905. A beautiful blessing and very interesting.

Discussed the effects and feelings generated by some of the ladies at what is said to be a private meeting held each Thursday night at Arnold Boss'.

Marion had to leave early so circle prayer was formed with John as mouth. Also closed the meeting.

149 B ☙

Monday, May 26, 1941.
Place: 744 East South.
Time: 9:00 a.m.

Present: John, Joseph, Charles, Louis, Roy, and Marion. John presided and Joseph conducted.

Joseph gave a financial report on the farming program. Receipts $150. Disbursements $108. The effort is not progressing as rapidly as hoped.

The saints, both in Idaho and California, have been asking for some of the brethren to come visit them.

John moved we take the Idaho trip Friday morning (May 23). Unanimously approved.

Brother Francis M. Darter is lecturing Sunday June 1, 1941 on one of his very favorite subjects – "Darter's answer to the Kingdom Group regarding Keys of the Priesthood now with Indians." Lyman Jessop and Rulon Allred are to be asked to attend the lecture and give a report thereof. A copy of Brother Darter's notice of his lecture follows these minutes.

Marion is to approach John Butcherite and feel out his spirit with the view in mind of inviting him to attend the special priesthood meetings held with the brethren once a month.

Sacrament administered by Charles and Marion.

Discussed matter of current interest.

John closed, being mouth for the prayer circle.

A

B

C

N

O

P

Q

R

S

T

U

V

W

Y

Z

Remaining Coded Entries

Made in the USA
Coppell, TX
28 January 2023